More Praise for Data

MW01004968

"As we enter into the era of Common Core, the need to view data in an organic and systemic lens is required to understand future trends and student needs. Datnow and Park introduce the four Ps context-focused approach to understanding the implementation of data use, which enables district leaders and teachers to move beyond simple questions of whether it is effective or useful for teaching and learning. This book is a must read for schools and districts ready to move beyond the PLC paradigm."

—Francisco Escobedo, superintendent,
Chula Vista Elementary School District

"Wisdom and experience are what set this book apart. Datnow and Park have the wisdom to recognize that successful data use is less about technology and more about integrating it into the everyday practices of schools. And they have the experience, drawn from their careful studies of how real schools and districts use data, to describe the essential conditions necessary to harness the power of data. If you're looking for practical insights into how data can make a difference in your organization, this book is an essential resource."

—Jonathan Supovitz, co-director, Consortium
for Policy Research in Education, and
associate professor, Graduate School of
Education, University of Pennsylvania

The Jossey-Bass
Leadership Library in Education

———

Andy Hargreaves

Consulting Editor

THE JOSSEY-BASS LEADERSHIP LIBRARY IN EDUCA-
TION is a distinctive series of original, accessible,
and concise books designed to address some of
the most important challenges facing educational
leaders. Its authors are respected thinkers in the
field who bring practical wisdom and fresh insight
to emerging and enduring issues in educational
leadership. Packed with significant research, rich
examples, and cutting-edge ideas, these books will
help both novice and veteran leaders understand
their practice more deeply and make schools better
places to learn and work.

ANDY HARGREAVES is the Thomas More Brennan
Chair in Education in the Lynch School of
Education at Boston College. He is the author of
numerous books on culture, change, and leadership in education.

For current and forthcoming titles in the series,
please see the last page of this book.

Titles in the Jossey-Bass Leadership Library in Education Series

STUDENT-CENTERED LEADERSHIP
Viviane Robinson * ISBN 978–0–47087413–4

WOMEN AND EDUCATIONAL LEADERSHIP
Margaret Grogan and Charol Shakeshaft *
ISBN 978–0–470–47043–5

URBAN SCHOOL LEADERSHIP
Tom Payzant * ISBN 978–0–7879–8621–6

TURNAROUND LEADERSHIP
Michael Fullan * ISBN 978–0–7879–6985–1

DISTRIBUTED LEADERSHIP
James Spillane * ISBN 978–0–7879–6538–9

INCLUSIVE LEADERSHIP
James Ryan * ISBN 978–0–7879–6508–2

SUSTAINABLE LEADERSHIP
Andy Hargreaves and Dean Fink *
ISBN 978–0–7879–6838–0

ETHICAL LEADERSHIP
Robert J. Starratt * ISBN 978–0–7879–6564–8

TEACHER LEADERSHIP
Ann Lieberman and Lynne Miller *
ISBN 978–0–7879–6245–6

DATA-DRIVEN LEADERSHIP
Amanda Datnow and Vicki Park *
ISBN 978–0–470–59479–7

Data-Driven Leadership

Amanda Datnow
Vicki Park

JB JOSSEY-BASS™
A Wiley Brand

Cover design by Jeff Puda
Cover image: © Thinkstock

Copyright © 2014 by John Wiley & Sons, Inc. All rights reserved.

Published by Jossey-Bass
A Wiley Brand
One Montgomery Street, Suite 1200, San Francisco, CA 94104-4594—www.josseybass.com

No part of this publication may be reproduced, stored in a retrieval system, or transmitted in any form or by any means, electronic, mechanical, photocopying, recording, scanning, or otherwise, except as permitted under Section 107 or 108 of the 1976 United States Copyright Act, without either the prior written permission of the publisher, or authorization through payment of the appropriate per-copy fee to the Copyright Clearance Center, Inc., 222 Rosewood Drive, Danvers, MA 01923, 978-750-8400, fax 978-646-8600, or on the Web at www.copyright.com. Requests to the publisher for permission should be addressed to the Permissions Department, John Wiley & Sons, Inc., 111 River Street, Hoboken, NJ 07030, 201-748-6011, fax 201-748-6008, or online at www.wiley.com/go/permissions.

Limit of Liability/Disclaimer of Warranty: While the publisher and author have used their best efforts in preparing this book, they make no representations or warranties with respect to the accuracy or completeness of the contents of this book and specifically disclaim any implied warranties of merchantability or fitness for a particular purpose. No warranty may be created or extended by sales representatives or written sales materials. The advice and strategies contained herein may not be suitable for your situation. You should consult with a professional where appropriate. Neither the publisher nor author shall be liable for any loss of profit or any other commercial damages, including but not limited to special, incidental, consequential, or other damages. Readers should be aware that Internet Web sites offered as citations and/or sources for further information may have changed or disappeared between the time this was written and when it is read.

Jossey-Bass books and products are available through most bookstores. To contact Jossey-Bass directly call our Customer Care Department within the U.S. at 800-956-7739, outside the U.S. at 317-572-3986, or fax 317-572-4002.

Wiley publishes in a variety of print and electronic formats and by print-on-demand. Some material included with standard print versions of this book may not be included in e-books or in print-on-demand. If this book refers to media such as a CD or DVD that is not included in the version you purchased, you may download this material at **http://booksupport.wiley.com**. For more information about Wiley products, visit **www.wiley.com**.

Library of Congress Cataloging-in-Publication Data has been applied for and is on file with the Library of Congress.

ISBN 978-0-470-59479-7 (pbk); ISBN 978-1-118-22060-3 (ebk);
ISBN 978-1-118-23408-2 (ebk)

Printed in the United States of America
FIRST EDITION
PB Printing   10 9 8 7 6 5 4 3 2 1

Contents

The Authors

Amanda Datnow is a professor in the Department of Education Studies at the University of California, San Diego, where she also served as department chair. Since receiving her PhD at UCLA, she has spent the past two decades conducting research on educational reform, particularly focusing on issues of equity and the professional lives of educators. Her goals are to both improve policy and practice in education and advance theory about educational change. She is the author or editor of seven books and over sixty articles and book chapters.

Vicki Park is an assistant professor in the Department of Educational Leadership, Connie L. Lurie College of Education at San José State University. Her work broadly focuses on urban school reform, data-informed leadership for equity, and the ways in which class, race, and gender shape the academic development of low-income youth. She earned her PhD in urban education policy with an emphasis on K–12 leadership and administration from the University of Southern California. Prior to earning her doctorate, she worked as an elementary and middle school teacher in California.

Acknowledgments

Some of the work reported in this book was supported by a grant from the NewSchools Venture Fund, with funding received from the Bill & Melinda Gates Foundation and the William and Flora Hewlett Foundation. We are grateful to our colleagues at NewSchools for assisting us in this effort. However, the contents of this book do not necessarily reflect the positions or policies of NewSchools or of the foundations.

We express our sincere thanks to the incredibly thoughtful, committed, and pioneering educators who gave generously of their time and effort to participate in this study. We also thank our research team colleagues at the Center on Educational Governance at the University of Southern California. We acknowledge the anonymous reviewers for their thoughtful feedback on an earlier version and, most notably, Andy Hargreaves, the series editor, for his tremendous insights that helped us transform our writing. We also wish to thank our former and current students, as these highly committed educators help enlighten us about the daily successes and challenges of using data in educational improvement. We give special thanks to Karen Jarsky for her superb editing of this manuscript. Finally, we thank Marjorie McAneny and Kate Gagnon at Jossey-Bass for supporting us in moving this book to completion.

Chapter 1

The Promise and Pitfalls of Data-Driven Decision Making

Data are ubiquitous in our lives. Using the latest technologies, we can now quickly calculate how many steps we took in a day, how many calories we consumed, and how much money we spent and on what. Knowing this information will ideally help us make better decisions that will improve the quality of our lives. Businesses, health and education organizations, and governments can now quickly crunch big data to help them understand phenomena in ways never before possible.[1] The power of data use is simple: armed with data, people will make better choices and organizations will function more effectively. This is the thinking behind a hot topic in educational reform: data-driven decision making.

A decade ago, data-driven decision making wasn't on the radar of most educators or policymakers. Now it is difficult to imagine an educational reform agenda that does not include data use as a key pillar. The use of data has the potential to change teaching and learning. Teachers now have wider access to information about students' learning and can address learning gaps before students fall behind. Data use can also build collective responsibility for all students. As student achievement results and teaching strategies are shared among teachers within and across grades, school cultures and routines are changing as well. Transparency is increasing and the culture of individualism that used to characterize classroom teaching is decreasing.

But how do we find the time to incorporate data use into the already incredibly busy professional lives of leaders and teachers?

What gets pushed aside if teachers focus on data? How much training and support do educators need to use data effectively? How does data use fit with other reform agendas? Are we in danger of chasing the numbers and forgetting the central purpose of data use, which is to improve teaching and learning?

> *Are we in danger of chasing the numbers and forgetting the central purpose of data use, which is to improve teaching and learning?*

Are we in danger of chasing the numbers and forgetting the central purpose of data use, which is to improve teaching and learning? Data-driven decision making is very popular in schools and districts across the United States, and there is also increasing emphasis on data use in other countries, including the Netherlands, Canada, Belgium, South Africa, Australia, and New Zealand.[2] Although each place may take a different approach, the common idea is that when leaders and teachers become knowledgeable about how to use data in their work—when they collect and analyze data to guide educational decisions—they will become more effective in reviewing their existing capacities, identifying weaknesses, and charting plans for improvement. In the classroom, data can inform how teachers plan lessons, identify concepts for reteaching, and differentiate instruction.[3]

The push for educators to systematically gather and use data has brought with it a need to develop new competencies, skills, and cultures. But using data is not as straightforward as it seems. Leadership is essential in this endeavor. We can't simply use data and expect good things to happen. Educational leaders play a critical role in shaping how and why data are used, what counts as data, and what people are aiming for when they push the use of data in schools. Although we titled this book *Data-Driven Leadership*, we strongly believe that data do not drive decisions by themselves. Individuals use data to engage in inquiry around current practices and inform courses of action. *Data-informed leadership* is thus a more appropriate term for what we're asking leaders to do.[4] And although the term *data-driven decision making* is commonly used in the field, from here onward we will refer to the practice as *data-informed decision making* to signal this important shift in thinking about data use. Leaders, we argue, should use data carefully to inform thoughtful decision making as part of an ongoing process of continuous improvement. Data use should not be seen as a passing fad or fancy. Leaders must take the initiative to assess what types of data are useful and for what purposes. Data-informed leadership aims to contribute to improving student achievement and teacher professionalism rather than threatening them.[5]

This book is written primarily for educational leaders at the school and district levels. It is geared toward leaders who are interested in becoming more data informed, as well as those who are well on the way and already feeling confident in their approach. Our aim is to provide a guide that will help build the reflective skills of leaders rather than offer a set of prescriptions about putting data use into practice. In order to help leaders get smarter about data use, we share research-based lessons learned from educators about how they have approached data use in their school systems. We examine how district and school leaders can create structures and cultures that support thoughtful engagement with data for continuous improvement. We also expose some of the potential land mines on the road to productive use of data for continuous learning and equity. Our intention is to help leaders avoid those problems and use data effectively and strategically in their decision making.

Perils and Perverse Incentives

All schools are already data informed in one sense or another. In the United States, the existing accountability system and its evaluation of schools based on student performance data expects and ensures it. Behind government accountability policies is the notion that educators need to know how to analyze, interpret, and use data so that they can make informed decisions about how to improve student achievement on state or national assessments. Within this, there is a strong policy emphasis on reducing the achievement gap, especially for historically underserved, low-income students of color.

Data can be very powerful, but they also have hazards.[6] There are some perverse incentives inherent in using accountability data within a high-stakes, limited-resource environment, which have led to some perilous practices and pitfalls, including these:

- Cheating on state tests
- Implementing quick fixes
- Targeting resources to students just below accountability thresholds
- Narrowing the curriculum
- Data overload

Cheating on State Tests

Accountability policies "invest faith in ever-increasing and voluminous amounts of numerical data collection. They can create an evidence base for an Orwellian system that can see everything, know everyone, and judge just when and where to intervene with any student, school or classroom, at any time."[7] Continual surveillance and high-stakes tests have resulted in a great deal of fear among many educators struggling to help their students show progress on state tests. In some cases, teachers and administrators have resorted to outright cheating by giving students the answers or changing students' answers after they have completed the tests, before they are sent for scoring.[8]

Implementing Quick Fixes

Critics argue that the term *data-driven decision making* implies an overly technical model of professional action in which educators diagnose weaknesses and implement solutions in a linear fashion, ignoring the complexity of the teaching and learning process.[9] As Andy Hargreaves and Dennis Shirley claim, this kind of focus on data use through numerical test score data can impair and impede the improvement of learning for all students:

> With AYP [Adequate Yearly Progress] deadlines looming and time running out, teachers have little chance to consider how best to respond to figures in front of them. They find themselves instead scrambling to apply instant solutions to all the students in the problematic cells—extra test-prep, new prescribed programs, or after-school and Saturday school sessions. There are few considered, professional developments here, just simplistic solutions driven by the scores and the political pressures behind them.[10]

This approach can lead to a focus on easy solutions rather than continuous development and substantive improvements.

Targeting Students Just below Accountability Thresholds

Accountability policies are meant to ensure that educators have high expectations for all students. They are intended to raise achievement across the board, regardless of students' current ability levels. In what has been graphically termed "educational triage,"[11] some schools separate students they see as "nonurgent" from those who are "suitable for treatment" and those who are seen as hopeless cases.[12] This is done in order to target resources and attention more economically and address the increasing emphasis on accountability. Educators frequently report focusing their efforts on students who are hovering near the cutoff point for proficiency.[13] Teachers target for remediation and additional tutoring those on the cusp—or "bubble"—of scoring in the proficient range while the students below this level are sometimes considered lost causes.[14] Similarly, observations of teachers' data reflection meetings in four schools revealed that discussions overwhelmingly centered on helping students who were below proficiency levels, with few discussions on raising students from proficient to advanced.[15] Other research has also indicated that school-level administrators frequently feel pressure from their districts to use data reports to target "bubble kids."[16] The resulting focus on specific groups of students at the expense of others has important implications for equity, especially with regard to equal opportunity to learn.

Narrowing of the Curriculum

A commonly documented concern arising from accountability policies is the narrowing of the curriculum. High-stakes testing has been found to sway schools to focus on math and language arts at the expense of other subjects, such as science or social studies.[17] This occurs even when principals provide support for teacher professionalism and autonomy in instructional decision making.[18] Some subjects get squeezed out altogether, and within targeted subjects, such as math and language arts, educators may spend their time teaching how to take tests—by emphasizing the styles and formats of state assessments, for example—rather than on what will be tested.[19] Such strategies may produce short-term gains on test scores, but students ultimately learn less because testing mastery is emphasized over learning.

Data Overload

The data collected and the expectations for using the data can far outweigh the supports necessary to make data use meaningful for instructional improvement and school change. Many schools are still at the basic stage of data use, relying on limited forms of data and simple processes of analysis.[20] Yet school leaders are saturated with accountability data from state and federal systems and district benchmark assessments, schoolwide data on student and teacher performance, and data on school culture, pacing, curriculum, and resource allocation, not to mention data from research and program evaluations. When school administrators and teachers are drowning in a sea of data and lack the capacity to use them, they are more likely to discount data altogether or fall into a default mode of quick-fix decision making without incorporating new evidence.[21]

When educators are overloaded or focus on the use of data to avoid sanctions, they may inadvertently subvert the intended goals of data use and accountability policies. With these perils and perverse incentives in mind, let's turn our attention to the promise of data use—the positives it can bring.

The Promise of Data Use for Equity and Excellence

There are many pitfalls of data use associated with mandated accountability policies but also a great deal of promise. Given the high-stakes context, it is easy to conflate and confuse data use with testing and testing data, but the two are not the same. The push for data use for educational improvement precedes the high-stakes accountability movement; it can be found much earlier in reforms such as Total Quality Management, continuous improvement, and the effective schools movement, among others. The type of data use that is connected to accountability is narrowly construed in terms of what and how data are used, but other and better possibilities also exist. Thus, we should not confuse data use with accountability or assume that the two must be linked. We believe there is value in using data as part of a broader school improvement process and to help create more equitable schools. In fact, a school improvement process in which various forms of evidence about student learning do not play a prominent role would be misguided.

The time is right for this. Across the globe, there are examples of efforts to engage students in deeper learning, more critical thinking, and the development of other twenty-first-century skills. The implementation of the Common Core State Standards in most US states has dramatic implications for how students will learn and how we will measure their progress. In the near future, we might reasonably expect to see more students taking increased responsibility for setting goals for their learning, see more teachers functioning as facilitators, and find more activities within schools that promote discovery of knowledge. To teach in these ways, educators will need to develop learning outcomes that are based in what students should know and be able to do. But broader learning goals do not necessarily lend themselves to easy measurement or analysis. What counts as "data" has to go beyond achievement scores, and we must move beyond narrow assessments of student achievement.

Why should leaders be data informed? What is the promise of data use, according to researchers? Studies on data use in education suggest that it can have a positive effect on school improvement.[22] The use of data by teachers in particular can be beneficial to instruction and student learning in the following ways:

- Data can help teachers set and refine concrete goals.[23]

- Data can help teachers decide how to pace their instruction, align their lessons to standards, identify lessons for reteaching, guide flexible grouping of students, and target students for intervention.[24]

- Data can enable teachers to pinpoint instructional strengths and weaknesses and encourage them to share best practices.[25]

- Data can be used to shed light on discrepancies between grades and assessments, which can indicate when there is a need to reexamine grading practices.

- Data use can foster a culture of inquiry and reinforce school priorities because the information aids communication among teachers, students, parents, and the rest of the school community.[26]

From an equity standpoint, when educators are confronted with evidence that challenges their views about students' abilities, data can act as a potential catalyst for changing perceptions.[27] Thus, the use of data may help contest negative tacit beliefs and assumptions about low-income students and students of color. In one study, when teachers in lower-achieving schools were able to make comparisons between their own data and data from high-performing schools with similar student demographics, they stopped blaming students' backgrounds for low academic results.[28] In another study, the emphasis on disaggregating student data by subgroups in the state's accountability system helped to displace (but not totally eliminate) deficit views of students.[29] And when educators at a high school reviewed the relationship between student assessment data and student absence data, it challenged their beliefs that student absence led to poor academic performance: "When data revealed false assumptions or hunches about specific groups of students, it became easier to get school staff to recognize the importance of basing decisions on data."[30] In short, when confronted with data, teachers are given empirical information to engage in conversations on improving both student engagement and the quality of instruction.

When the focus is on organizational learning and student achievement, data use practices may positively influence continuous improvement efforts. This type of use is not characterized by sporadic examination of test results, but rather by systematic and sustained reflection on a multiple array of indicators. If data use is central in the school planning and improvement process, it becomes infused into the structure and culture of the organization. Mutually supportive structures, policies, and technical capacities embedded within this culture of collaborative inquiry are necessary if data are to become a relevant and useful for improving teaching and student learning.

What Counts as Data?

Data use can take many different forms depending on what data are used, for what purposes, and by whom. In some districts, data use is synonymous with the examination of annual state test score data. In others, data use involves examination and action planning around score reports from benchmark assessment tests administered several times a year. Principals and teachers review these reports to help them identify which students are performing above, at, or below grade level relative to state standards. Teachers may analyze data individually or with other teachers in grade-level or subject-area teams in order to target instructional support toward the students who score below grade level. Although at first glance this may appear to be a fairly narrow use of data to inform instructional decision making, in reality it is likely far less technical and linear than it seems. Teachers may develop their own common assessments and gather together in professional learning communities to assess student progress and plan next steps. They may also bring examples of student work (e.g., homework, writing samples) to the table, as well as their own professional knowledge, as they plan for instruction.

But data-informed decision making need not rely only on student outcome data. Educators may also examine student demographic data, data on implementation or progress toward goals, survey data from students or parents, and classroom observation data. In some schools, student behavior and discipline data are also considered to be important elements in improving learning and instruction. In schools, data are typically categorized into four main types:

1. *Demographic data,* including attendance and discipline records
2. *Student achievement data,* which encompass not only standardized test data but also formative assessments, teacher-developed assessments, writing portfolios, and running records

3. *Instructional data*, which include teachers' use of time, patterns of course enrollment, and the quality of the curriculum

4. *Perception data*, which provide insights regarding values, beliefs, and views of individuals or groups (e.g., surveys, focus groups)[31]

These varied forms of data are useful for a range of purposes. In this book, we refer to data that inform teachers about their teaching and the learning of their students and, to a lesser extent, to data that inform school and system leaders about improvement more generally.

Data from assessments may show patterns of student achievement, but they do not tell teachers what to do differently in the classroom.[32] And large-scale assessment data may be useful for school and system planning, but they are less useful at the teacher or student level.[33] So while the heavy emphasis on accountability may have saturated schools with a wide array of data, educators are still figuring out how to develop the skills to use those data in both basic and more sophisticated ways.

When districts and schools begin to define what *data* or *evidence* means in their local settings, a more complex definition of student learning goals emerges. Even prior to any mention of the new Common Core Standards in the United States, we found that districts relied on a broad range of evidence to inform decision making, including standardized assessments, placement data, benchmarks, observational data, and other sources at the system and school levels. Some forerunner districts are gathering and analyzing data on the extent of student engagement in order to improve student involvement in their own learning.[34] These findings are particularly pertinent to the work of district and school leaders who will be thinking about new ways to measure and track student learning.

What Is Data-Informed Decision Making?

The term *data-informed* (or *data-driven*) *decision making* is sufficiently vague to be a catchphrase for all things having to do with data. With the presence of accountability systems that are so closely tied to test scores, schools and districts are likely to consider themselves data informed whether or not they desire to be so. Reports of high-performing schools and districts engaging in data-informed decision making persuade some leaders to embrace data use, even though the strategy itself may not be completely defined.[35] Getting clearer on what data-informed decision making is—and is not—is essential.

Some who seek to define *data use* focus on information processing of data. According to Mandinach and Honey's model, individuals collect and organize data—as raw pieces of facts.[36] The raw facts become information when individuals analyze and summarize them. In other words, information is data with meaning, and it becomes knowledge when the information is synthesized and prioritized. Thus, knowledge is essentially information that has been deemed useful to guide action. Figure 1.1 depicts this model of data use. This information model is helpful because it lays out the stages of data use and highlights that it is not a simple process of having and then using data. This is a critical piece of the puzzle in conceptualizing data use. Instead, data must be interpreted and knowledge must be actively constructed in order for the data to affect decisions. The model also highlights the fact that data use at the classroom level is embedded in the larger context of the school and the district. But there are some aspects of data-informed decision making that this model doesn't capture because, of course, no one model can capture everything. Different levels of capacity may shape educators' abilities to engage in the process of transforming data into knowledge. In addition, educators' beliefs and assumptions likely shape their interpretations of data, and their ability to use data may be enabled or constrained by these factors. For these reasons, data use is not likely to be an entirely sequential process, since it varies a great deal with the context.

Another data use model concentrates on educators' abilities and capacities to use data. This learning model, described by Earl and Katz, recognizes that schools and individuals may have

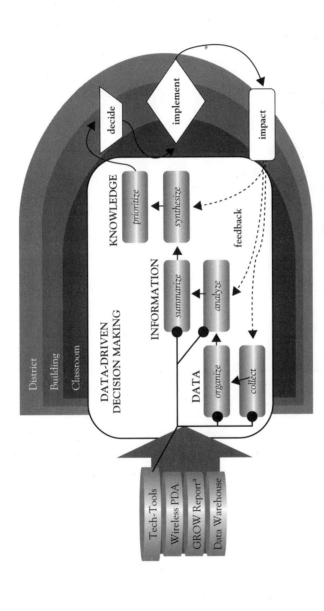

Figure 1.1.   Sequential Model of Data Use

[a]Reprinted by permission of Publisher. From Ellen B. Mandinach and Margaret Honey, eds., *Data-Driven School Improvement: Linking Data and Learning*, New York: Teachers College Press. Copyright © 2008 by Teachers College, Columbia University. All rights reserved.[37]

13

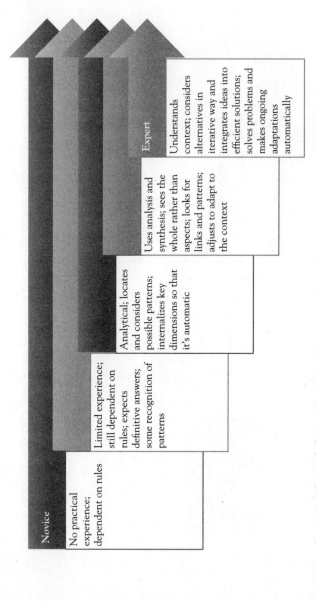

Figure 1.2. Stages in Growth from Novice to Expert in Data Use

Source: Adapted from L. Earl and S. Katz, *Leading Schools in a Data-Rich World: Harnessing Data for School Improvement* (Thousand Oaks, CA: Corwin Press, 2006), 102.

The text within the figure, from the lowest to highest stage:

Novice
No practical experience; dependent on rules

Limited experience; still dependent on rules; expects definitive answers; some recognition of patterns

Analytical; locates and considers possible patterns; internalizes key dimensions so that it's automatic

Uses analysis and synthesis; sees the whole rather than aspects; looks for links and patterns; adjusts to adapt to the context

Expert
Understands context; considers alternatives in iterative way and integrates ideas into efficient solutions; solves problems and makes ongoing adaptations automatically

different levels of expertise when it comes to thoughtfully using data. Because of the developmental process, educators require opportunities to learn and apply their skills. This conceptualization underlines how data use is not just a sequential process of finding and using information, but one of skill and learning. Figure 1.2 lists the stages of the model, which together highlight the developmental nature of using data.

This model helps us understand the continuum of skills in learning to use data, which is also part of the puzzle. However, it does not address how the development of skills is supported or hindered by conditions in local educational settings, an issue we take up explicitly in this book.

> *This model helps us understand the continuum of skills in learning to use data, which is also part of the puzzle.*

A third model, presented by Gina Ikemoto and Julie Marsh, blends aspects of these first two models, focusing on the capacity of schools to engage in data use and the range of related processes that educators may undertake. This model presents two overlapping continuums having to do with the relative complexity of data types and of data analysis and decision making. Data complexity has to do with a range of factors, including the time frame of the data, the type of data, the data source, and the level of detail of the data. The relative complexity of data analysis and decision making relates to how the data are interpreted. In other words:

- Are analyses based on assumptions or empirical evidence?
- Are they rooted in basic or expert knowledge?
- Are analysis techniques straightforward or sophisticated?
- Are decisions made individually or collectively?
- Are they rooted in single or iterative processing?[38]

Depending on the balance of the complexity of the data and the complexity of data analysis and decision making, a school

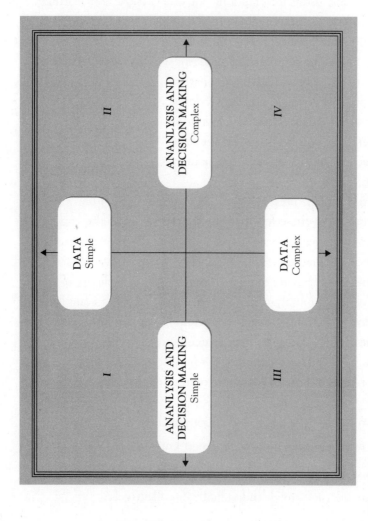

Figure 1.3. Framework for Simple versus Complex Data-Driven Decision Making

Source: G. S. Ikemoto and J. A. Marsh, "Cutting through the 'Data Driven' Mantra: Different Conceptions of Data-Driven Decision Making," *Yearbook of the National Society for the Study of Education, 106* (2007): 105–131. Reprinted with permission from Gina Ikemoto and Julie Marsh.

may be considered basic, analysis focused, data focused, or inquiry focused. Figure 1.3 depicts this model.

Schools that fell in the basic category tended to use simple data and engage in simple analysis. For instance, a principal in one school noticed students didn't perform well on the state test in mathematics and scheduled professional development. In other words, only one person at just one point in time used only one source of data. Analysis-focused schools also focused on the collection of simple data, but they undertook complex analysis and decision making collectively. Data-focused schools collected complex data but engaged in simple analysis. For example, one school brought a group together to look at a range of data on student learning, but they didn't draw on empirical or expert knowledge to analyze the data. Inquiry-focused schools collected complex data and employed complex analysis and decision making. These schools drew on multiple sources of data and examined evidence collectively over a period of time in order to address a particular problem of practice. They also integrated the knowledge of experts. Although the majority of schools that took part in the study that informed this model described their practices as falling in the basic category, in reality they covered the full range, from basic to inquiry-focused models of data use.

It is useful to consider this entire range of data use models because it underscores the importance of examining how different contextual factors may influence how schools use data. Ultimately the model makes clear that data use is not a straightforward process and no single model is the ideal type; rather, different models may be useful for different purposes and in different places.

Our own research and the work of other scholars suggest that all three of these models have relevance. In other words, we need a clear understanding of how data are conceptualized and used in specific contexts because individual schools are at different stages of implementation and have different models of data collection and use. There is no singular theory or model of data use for decision making. An emphasis on evidence-based practice and the capacity to engage in data use need to be considered within specific organizations and in light of the larger policy environment because both of these factors structure how data are used and for what purposes. Our purpose is to consider the role of leadership in creating a supportive structure and culture that engages teachers in capacity-building efforts. The ways in which these elements work to reinforce or undermine the relevance of data use have important implications for the effectiveness of using data for educational improvement.

The Critical Role of Data-Informed Leadership

Leaders play a key role in realizing the goals of an inquiry-informed data use process that is reliant on a wide range of data sources for the purpose of improving student learning. They also face numerous challenges, in part because they must establish cultures and structures that support data use and build teachers' capacity to use data in a way that will inform thoughtful instructional changes. Leadership is a crucial bridge that can support and direct these new learning efforts.[39]

As we mentioned earlier, we advocate for data-*informed* leadership, not data-*driven* leadership. This reflects our belief that data do not drive courses of action but rather provide the starting point for inquiry.[40] Data will not and should not tell us everything, and not all data should drive instructional changes. Data can inform school, district, and classroom planning, but some forms of data are better suited for planning at one level than another.[41] One of the most important jobs a leader undertakes with respect to data use is asking the right questions. By asking the right questions and framing the process of data use in a particular way, leaders shape the perceptions and outcomes of data use within their school systems.[42]

Data-informed leadership is a shared enterprise. In the past, individualized accounts of leaders tended to dominate research on educational leadership.[43] But tackling the complex dilemmas of school improvement today requires that we move away from a reliance on exceptional principals or individual expert teachers. Indeed, research on

> *Data will not and should not tell us everything, and not all data should drive instructional changes.*

educational leadership has moved beyond an individualistic, role-embedded conceptualization of leadership and leadership practices to one that focuses more broadly on shared knowledge, expertise, and action.[44] Data-informed leadership is shared among school and district leaders in formal positions, as well as teacher leaders in informal positions. Individual leaders still matter, but what matters more is how they relate to and work with others. In schools and districts, leaders primarily exert their influence by setting directions for school improvement, cultivating shared goals and norms, developing human capacity, and modifying structures to create conditions that support student achievement.[45]

With these new directions for educational leadership, notions of what it means to lead have also evolved. A new focus on cognitive frameworks based on constructivist learning theories recognizes that people actively construct knowledge and that learning is an interactive process situated in specific social contexts.[46] Therefore, any reform effort must take into account how teachers and administrators make sense of policy and actions.[47] In other words, leaders should actively construct interpretations of school improvement that foster student *and* educator learning and develop conditions that support such efforts. We delve into this in more detail in chapter 3.

As we focus on the cognitive dimensions of what it means to lead, the concept of distributed leadership offers a useful framework for our investigation of data use. It moves away from viewing leadership as an inherent property of someone in a formal role and toward an understanding that leadership operates within a network of people with shared and complementary knowledge and expertise.[48] As a result, the distributed leadership perspective does not focus solely on the individual principal or teacher but rather on the actions of a group working together.[49] The focus is on the social interaction among people within a school or district rather than just the acts of one person. Thus, in data-informed leadership, we advocate for interdependency among educators, dispersed responsibilities, and reciprocity among individuals rather than relationships of control and compliance.[50] The distributed leadership perspective is essential for data-informed leadership, as this reform relies on the strengths and skills of a variety of people in a school and district.

Numerous studies have explored the distributed leadership perspective, but most have concentrated at the school level without analyzing how district leadership may shape school-level leadership styles, processes, and practices.[51] The emphasis on data use for educational improvement is an ideal reform context in which to examine these particular dynamics since both school- and district-level leadership are critical in data use efforts. School systems play an increasingly pivotal role in leadership and collaboration with school sites to make data use an engine of reform. Inclusiveness in using data to make decisions is often prevalent.

In districts that support data use for decision making, the superintendent and school board members often know how to lead and support data use. These districts may have staff members who work as liaisons with principals and individual schools.[52] Districts and schools may also be shifting the focus of their professional development practices from compliance to support in order to build the skills of their staff to participate in decision-making processes and create an organizational culture of inquiry. Not only are principals privy to repositories of assessment data, but just as important, so are teachers, and they are encouraged to take a close look at grade-level and classroom data and to share and discuss the data with each other in order to make instructional choices.[53]

Overall, while the literature confirms the importance of effective leadership,[54] the emerging research on the implementation of data-informed decision making suggests that the relationships between districts and schools and between principals and teachers are changing.[55] Given the increasing interdependency between districts and schools as they lead data-informed decision-making practices, it is important to unpack how leadership practices are being changed and how they are changing reform efforts.

The concept of data-informed leadership centers on an activity system of people and their ways of working within a specific school or district context. In this book, we are guided by this theory of distributed leadership as we analyze the connections between district- and school-level data-informed decision making and leadership practices. We explain how leaders at the district level build a common interpretation of and orientation toward data use for decision making, which are then mediated at the school level by formal and informal leaders. From this framework, our book focuses on how data-informed leadership plays a role in the use of data in schools and districts. More specifically, we address the following questions:

- How do the people, policies, practices, and patterns in a school shape data-informed decision making?

- How can district and school leaders cultivate a culture of data-informed decision making?

- How can goals, tools, and routines enable data-informed decision making?

- How can leaders support teachers in engaging in data-informed decision making?

- What is the impact of data use on instructional practice?

The Knowledge Base for This Book

This book draws primarily on a national, multisite case study on the implementation of data use in high-performing, diverse urban school systems. The districts and schools we studied were chosen on the basis of their status as leaders in using data for instructional decision making and for their record of improved student achievement over time. In the chapters that follow, we present many research-based examples from our case study to illustrate the critical elements of data-informed decision making, as well as the role of data-informed leadership in fostering them. In many ways, the experiences of these schools and districts illustrate the promise of data use, but they do not give us much information about the pitfalls that many educators have encountered in their verve to adopt this reform. To illustrate more varied outcomes, we begin the next four chapters with vignettes from other places where the implementation and process of data-informed decision making have not been as smooth. These examples were gathered through our professional work with educators, and they should be viewed as hypothetical situations rather than as rigorous research examples. Nevertheless, they provide important counterpoints to the research findings we discuss and offer important lessons for data-informed leaders.

Organization of the Book

This book is organized around four major activities in data-informed leadership: knowing the context, reculturing, restructuring, and instructional change. In addressing these topics, we offer important lessons for educational leaders. At the end of each chapter, we conclude with reflective questions for leaders to consider on each topic. Our aim with this book is not to prescribe practices for leaders to follow but instead to help them think more critically about implementing data-informed decision making within their own specific schools and districts.

In chapter 2, we describe the importance of the educational setting—its people, policies, practices, and patterns of interaction—in reform more generally and in the process of data use in particular. We call on readers to use their knowledge of these "four Ps" in their own setting in order to plan successful change. We introduce the sites we studied, because understanding their contextual conditions is essential to learning from their successes. We describe each school system and its background in undertaking data-informed decision making as a key focus for improving student achievement and organizational learning.

In chapter 3, we draw on lessons from district and school leaders to explain how schools and systems can be "recultured" to enable effective data use. We explain how system and school leaders can work together to create explicit norms and expectations for continuous improvement, as well as engender a climate of trust so that teachers can openly discuss data. We discuss the explicit actions and activities by leaders at the school and district levels, collaboratively and individually, to accomplish the goal of reculturing through a new theory of action.

Chapter 4 focuses on the tools, routines, and resources that leaders engage to support data use. These include new ways of thinking about curriculum and assessments, new uses of time, new technologies, and the establishment of protocols for using data. As we describe these, we illuminate the trade-offs between centralization and decentralization and pressure and support.

Chapter 5 addresses the critical issue of supporting teachers to engage in inquiry around data for instructional decision making. Different educators can look at the same sets of data and draw rather different conclusions, and these differences can have important implications for equity and diversity. We describe the sources of data that the teachers at our research sites carefully reflected on in order to plan instructional changes, as well as the types of changes that they made. We reinforce the importance of building educators' skills to look at data, as well as their understanding of how their own levels of reflection shape what they see in the data and how they plan their actions accordingly.

In the final chapter, we conclude with concrete advice for data-informed leaders. We draw on the lessons from the book to provide seven specific calls to action with respect to data-informed leadership. We provide bold directions for leaders to reorient their leadership toward using data in ways that can strengthen teaching and learning for all students.

Our hope is that school and district leaders will find that the lessons in this book help them become more knowledgeable about data use. Data use is a critical component of educational improvement, and it should be an enduring feature, regardless of the reform being implemented. The success of data-informed decision making is a joint accomplishment of leaders who enable the practices of others across the system. Learning how to use data thoughtfully is not a one-time event or goal, but an evolving and dynamic process. This book will help leaders learn how to nurture a culture of data use and the structures that support it, from the district or principal's office to the classroom.

Chapter 2

The Four Ps of Educational Reform
People, Policies, Practices, and Patterns

It was the height of summer when James, an assistant principal, was charged with analyzing his middle school's test score data for the previous year and making recommendations to the principal. Two significant concerns quickly arose: seventh-grade math scores had declined by 15 percent since the previous year, and scores in eighth-grade history were down by 8 percent. The school was already under state sanction, and these declines would cause further concern at the district and state levels. James was not surprised. Last year he had observed and documented two problematic teaching situations in math and social studies. He observed a math teacher who seemed very disengaged and a history teacher who had little focus on academics. He had brought his concerns to his principal, who said he'd rather "wait until next year" to address the issues. But conversations with those teachers never occurred.

James believed his principal's pattern of avoiding conflict contributed to the decline in test scores. And he was frustrated that while his principal asked for his advice, he never followed it. James had some good ideas about how to address the issues arising from the data: changing the staffing in some classes, providing professional development to increase the use of formative assessments, and finding ways for instructional coaches to work better with teachers in need of support. Had his principal addressed the issues earlier, perhaps the students would have had a much better experience. However, not only did his formal position as an assistant principal limit his decision-making authority, but his informal relationship with the principal didn't allow for much influence either.

Using data to improve schools is not solely a technical practice or a logical, lockstep process. Many educators already use data to identify problems. Gaps in instructional practice can be obvious and well documented by student performance data and observations in the classroom. But crafting solutions and effecting change takes much more. The efforts of leaders to make data use relevant for school improvement are complex because they are situated in a setting governed by long-standing people, policies, practices, and patterns. These four Ps are critical to educational reform.

A Framework for Understanding Data Use: The Power of the Four Ps

Every school and district setting is distinct. A school has a unique set of leaders and teachers with established habits and patterns of interaction. One has only to witness the departure of a few key players to see how large an impact people have on a school. People also have particular patterns of interaction within a setting. In the same school, you can have a team of teachers that collaborates effectively to improve instruction alongside another that cannot stand to be in the same room together. In some schools, these teachers may wield a great deal of influence, whereas in others, they have very limited decision-making power. You may have a principal who confronts challenging problems or one whose style of avoidance or delay is the default mode of practice.

Policies shape the work of schools more than ever before, and districts are taking an increasingly active role in educational reform and accountability demands at governmental levels. At the school level, such policies help to inform classroom practices, as teachers emphasize certain content areas over others, group students in particular ways, and so on. Sometimes these practices occur for historical reasons. "That's the way we've always done things here," is a commonly heard phrase in schools.

The four Ps comprise the setting, or context, of educational change. The four Ps shape leaders' actions, how they think about their work, and even their level of commitment. The same is true for teachers. Lessons from decades of research and practice underscore that educational reform efforts cannot be fully understood unless their context is also understood. This is in marked contrast to earlier school reform that has been criticized for being insensitive to local conditions and factors, implying that recommendations for successful change could work in any school, at any time. Yet we know that people vary, places vary, and the ways in which people interact with the processes, tools, and artifacts that characterize educational reforms also vary. There may be some common patterns in how educational reform efforts unfold, but it has been well documented that the aspects of the local setting are critical and are intertwined with action at every moment in implementation.[1]

What this means for data-informed leadership is that we cannot fully evaluate whether tools or practices are effective in data use without knowing how they are used in schools, each with their own unique four Ps—for example:

> *We cannot fully evaluate whether tools or practices are effective in data use without knowing how they are used in schools.*

- An inquiry-based teacher team in one school may view a tool designed to facilitate their conversations about student achievement data as an inhibitor to progress, whereas a teacher team at another school that is not sure how to start the conversation may see it as a useful guide.

- In a public school, teaching may be constrained by institutional barriers such as state testing guidelines—guidelines that would not loom as large in a private school.

- In a community of politically savvy parents, the reform-minded actions of a group of teachers may be

questioned, but elsewhere parents might leave decisions to educators, allowing teachers to advance their
reform agenda.

By understanding the people, policies, practices, and patterns
in a school or district, we can better predict how reforms may play
out at the local level. Taking a broader perspective on data use,
the context-focused approach of the four Ps can help educators
more fully understand the complexities of the reform process.

The Four Ps Approach to Understanding Data-Informed Leadership

The context-focused approach of the four Ps to understanding
the implementation of data use enables researchers and practitioners to move beyond simple questions of whether it is effective
or useful for teaching and learning. It helps direct attention to
the people and conditions that shape the process and its potential consequences. Building on sociological theory, James Spillane
notes that differing rules and resources in, for example, a local
school or district setting can enable or constrain interactions. He
argues that we should study data use in terms of practice, which
he defines as the "more or less coordinated patterns and meaningful interactions of people at work."[2] We find meaning in these
practices by examining the setting in which they are situated.

If we look inside a school, we can see how protocols for doing
things, ways of talking about students, and norms of interaction
can help or constrain the data-informed leader. Sometimes the
same features simultaneously help and hinder. For example, grade-
level meetings afford opportunities for teachers to discuss data, but
they constrain opportunities for cross-grade conversations. So too,
standardized test data embody particular representations of what it
means to learn and teach. They define both teacher conversations
around data and the decisions and practices that result from those

data. State-level standardized assessments can create an urgency to focus on students' competencies in core subjects of English language arts and math while simultaneously reducing attention to other important subjects because they are not tested as often or at all.

Spillane's focus on organizational routines, daily interactions, and the importance of context as both an enabler and a constraint are consistent with our own earlier writing in which we reviewed the construction and sense-making perspectives on educational reform.[3] These theories help us further understand the four Ps. They provide us with a better understanding of why people respond to reform in different ways. We also learn how people, policies, practices, and their patterns of interaction dynamically interact to produce reform success or failure. These theories highlight the following important points:

- Reform implementation is not just a problem of will and organizational structure, but also one of social and individual learning. There is a range in how teachers and administrators view data. People's prior knowledge of and experiences with reform mediate how they respond to new initiatives. For example, teachers tend to focus on the aspects of new reforms that are familiar to them, perhaps leaving aside the aspects that are difficult to understand or implement.[4]

- Teachers engage in sense making individually and collectively.[5] Patterns of interaction among teachers influence how they adopt, adapt, or disregard reform initiatives, mediating the influence of these reforms on classroom practice. A tight group of experienced teachers may respond in similar ways to data use, and these ways may be quite different from the response by a group of new teachers. A group of math teachers may look at achievement data differently than a group of English teachers does.

- Power and politics come into play in educational reform.[6] We know from studies of school change that people in positions of power often have more opportunities to shape what is valued or privileged and what is discounted or suppressed.[7] To understand how people interact within a school setting, we also need to understand the role of power. In the case of data use, we look for examples of how district or school site leaders promote a model of data use that may or may not fit with teachers' needs, and we look for examples of superficial implementation of or outright resistance to mandates. Micropolitical dynamics such as these exist everywhere in school districts, and knowledge of how they shape reform is essential.

For these reasons, leaders play a key role in helping teachers find coherence among reforms and in helping them learn how to integrate them into their current practices. Investing in teachers' professional capital—their knowledge, understanding of how to work collaboratively, and skills in making wise judgments—is critical.[8] Hargreaves and Fullan call on leaders to build and circulate professional capital by changing the cultures of schools and districts.[9] Indeed, high-performing districts are characterized by a heavy investment in capacity building among leaders and teachers, particularly around instructional improvement.[10] The same is true at the school level. Across the globe, schools that are high performing are those that continually invest in building the skills of teachers.

These theoretical and empirical tools for understanding the people, policies, practices, and patterns within a setting remind us that leaders play an essential role in educational reform. They frame reform efforts and guide others in their sense making about those reforms. Leaders also mediate reforms and policies that originate at the state or federal levels. Data-informed leaders need to engage in all of these activities, as well as remain keenly aware of the local conditions that may help or hinder the work. They also need to be very knowledgeable about data use so that they can lead and model productive uses of data. This book provides lessons that assist data-informed leaders in these key areas.

Data-informed leadership cannot be divorced from the setting in which it is practiced because the context structures how data are actually used. In order to provide a foundation for the chapters that follow, we describe our data gathering in the sites we studied. Understanding the evidence base for the lessons in this book is critically important in order for data-informed leaders to learn how to successfully implement similar initiatives in their own sites.

> *Data-informed leadership cannot be divorced from the setting in which it is practiced.*

The Data Use Studies

The qualitative data for this book were gathered as part of a two-phase case study. We examined urban schools across the United States that exhibited positive outcomes related to their implementation of data-informed decision making. We recognize that data use efforts at the school level shape and are shaped by the school, district, state, and federal contexts. Educators interact with each other and with structures, skills, norms, and policies that exist within and across all of these levels. Figure 2.1 calls up many of the important elements that arise in data use efforts and fleshed out in this book:

- Student performance is at the heart of data-informed decision making.
- Numerous types of data can inform decisions.
- Tools can aid educators in gathering, analyzing, and using data effectively.
- Leadership stretches across districts and schools and helps shape the knowledge, skills, and capacity building for reform.

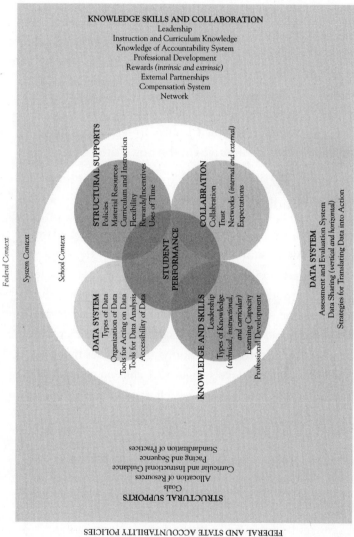

Figure 2.1.   Framework for Data-Informed Decision Making

Source: Adapted from A. Datnow, V. Park, and P. Wohlstetter, "Achieving with Data: How High Performing School Systems Use Data to Improve Instruction for Elementary School Students" (Oakland, CA: NewSchools Venture Fund, 2007).

32

- Knowledge and skill building around data use are required at both the school and district levels.

- Structural supports, collaboration, and capacity building are critical at both the district and school levels.

- Federal and state accountability policies can provide political leverage for district and school leaders to stimulate change, but they also serve as constraints.

The aim of our work was to expand knowledge about the processes and outcomes of data-informed decision making. Thus, we conducted case studies to capture the details of data use within numerous school and district contexts. A case study approach is useful when the boundaries between the topic under study and its context are not clearly distinguishable, as is certainly the case with educational reform in schools and districts.[11] The goal of this approach is to generalize to theoretical propositions, not to populations. We can't describe all schools and all educators, but we can build an understanding of data-informed leadership by looking carefully at sites where it was taking place.

Site Selection

We used purposive sampling to identify and select our research sites.[12] The funder of our study asked us to find locations that were:

- Leaders in the use of data

- Showed a record of improving student achievement over time

- Served student populations that were diverse in terms of race/ethnicity and socioeconomic status

To find sites that fit these criteria, we first conducted an Internet search of district websites looking for schools and districts that had won awards for improving achievement. We also examined research on data use, consulted with our funders, and asked for nominations from professional contacts in the fields of research, practice, and policy.

In the first phase of the research, we focused on districts as our entry point for the study because we were interested in how school systems support data use. At that stage, we had about twenty-five districts or charter management organizations that fit our criteria. Due to their unique nature and diverse structural arrangements, we do not draw on data we gathered from the charter management organization sites. We narrowed the list of possible sites after reviewing district and school websites, speaking with experts in the field, and conducting phone interviews with district leaders. We developed a set of initial questions for leaders to get a sense of the supports that were in place for data use—for example:

- Does your district have a data management system?
- Is there an expectation that teachers will use data to inform instructional decisions?
- Has the district provided training related to data use?

While they acknowledged the successes they had experienced in becoming more data informed, all of the leaders we spoke with were also careful to note that their work was "in progress." Once we chose the final districts, we asked each district superintendent to nominate the two schools under his or her jurisdiction that were furthest along in their use of data to inform decision making. Most of the sites in the first phase of our study were elementary schools.

In the second phase of the study, we used a similar process, but our focus was on finding schools (rather than districts) that were at the forefront with respect to data use. We identified fifty possible sites and then conducted a similar process of researching the sites and conducting phone interviews with principals to ask them a set of questions to ascertain how data were being used at their schools and what supports the school and district levels provided. Their answers allowed us to narrow the list.

Our analyses for this book drew on data collected in six public schools located in three districts in three states. For the purposes of confidentiality, we call them districts A, B, and C. (The appendix to this book provides an overview of the demographics of the sites.) All schools were racially diverse, though they served varied ethnic and racial populations. Three schools served the high school level; two served grades 9 through 12 and had student populations of about sixteen hundred that were racially diverse; one school served approximately nine hundred students just in grade 9. This unique structure was part of a district program to improve outcomes at the stage of transition to high school. The remaining three schools were midsize to large elementary schools. This mix of elementary and secondary schools provided an opportunity to see how differing school cultures and structures shaped teachers' data use.

Data Collection

Over several years, our team of researchers conducted two site visits to each location. During each visit, we spent two to three days at each school and visited district offices. We conducted the district office interviews primarily on the first site visit and the school interviews and observations on the second visit. The research team interviewed two or three district administrators, two or three administrators at each school site, and teachers across grade levels and academic disciplines. Most interviews lasted about an hour, though interviews with school and district leaders tended to be longer.

When we set up our site visits, we asked the principals to identify a variety of teachers in terms of interest in and engagement with data use. We invited the teachers they had recommended to be interviewed; sometimes these interviews led us to meet with other teachers who were not originally suggested by the principals. At each school, we attempted to include teachers from a mix of grade levels. At the high school level, we included teachers from a range of subject areas and also interviewed department chairs when possible. Ultimately the teachers we interviewed represented a wide range in terms of experience, age, gender, and racial background, as well as grade level and department and engagement with data use.

Across the three districts and six schools, we gathered data through the following:

- Nine interviews with district-level staff, including superintendents, assistant superintendents, and directors of research or assessment.

- Ten interviews with school site leaders—principals and assistant principals.

- Interviews with seventy-six teachers across the schools. Most of the teacher interviews were conducted individually but also some in small focus groups.

All of the interviews were recorded and transcribed verbatim.

At each school, we conducted informal observations of the school as a whole as well as classrooms and relevant meetings. We observed data discussions among teachers whenever possible so that we could capture data-informed instructional decision making in action. We do not have this information for all sites, however, because our visits sometimes did not coincide with such meetings. Thus, we do not draw on these data a great deal in this book. We gathered a plethora of documents at the school and system levels that were pertinent to our study (e.g., data discussion protocols, school improvement plans).

In keeping with our conceptual framework, we reviewed our transcripts, documents, and observational notes for general information on the system and school context for data use, any structural and cultural supports for data use, and any evidence of the impact of data use, among other categories. In doing so, we took note of how particular leadership activities and organizational features shaped educators' work with data. We coded the data according to these ideas and used the coded data to inform the development of a detailed case report for each school site. These reports aided us in identifying the cross-case themes we examine in this book.

Important Features of the Sites We Studied

Our research sites shared three important features with respect to people, policies, practices, and patterns. First, each was located in a state with a high-stakes accountability system. Each also had a history of stable and competent leadership, as well as a culture and structure that supported data use. These leadership and structural and cultural assets provided a positive climate for reform, and they also give an indication of the high level of capacity for reform at each of the sites. Of course, not all school sites have these characteristics; leaders who seek to undertake similar reform efforts would be wise to closely examine the features in their own schools and districts to ascertain the existing level of capacity in their own context and start from there. The lessons in this book will be useful to leaders trying to find inroads into developing such capacity. In either case, knowing the context is essential.

The People: A History of Stable Leadership

People are critical to the data-informed leadership stories we tell, as all three of the districts in our study had extremely stable and capable leaders. The superintendent in district A had been in that district for over twenty-five years by the time our study began, having worked her way up from being a student teacher. She was lauded by school personnel for providing strong, steady leadership for the district and for being supportive of school site autonomy and decision making. She believed in empowering individuals at all levels of the system and applied an incremental approach to change. She was careful to bring school site administrators and teachers along gently and to help them feel ownership of change efforts rather than imposing mandates from above that might produce resistance. The assistant superintendent for curriculum and instruction had also risen through the ranks and had been with the district for many years.

These patterns were also present in district B, where the current superintendent had been in place for ten years when our study began. As in district A, a large number of district personnel were former students or had come up through the ranks. Similarly, the superintendent of district C had been in the system for over forty years, first as a student and then as a teacher. She had been superintendent for six years when our study began. The director of curriculum had also worked her way up the system, having started as a teacher, and she had been in her position for five years when we met her. Not only did all of the districts have stable leadership and historical understanding of their organizations, but the leaders benefited from harmonious relationships with their governing boards and the local teachers' unions.

Leadership at the school site level was also mostly stable and strong. All but one of the principals had been at the respective school site for four years or more. All had extensive prior experience in education, and several also had experience working in other sectors, most notably the business sector. Some principals explained that their comfort in working with data was in part due to their previous experiences. By and large, principals in this study were well respected by school staff. Moreover, district leaders imbued principals with considerable autonomy in school site decision making as long as their decisions could be supported by data and they produced positive results. It is important to point out that we did not encounter any principals who felt hamstrung by district demands. This is most likely because of the parameters of our selection criteria and our relatively small sample size; we know there is a range of sentiments toward reform in any district.

All of the schools in our study had formal or informal leadership teams that were pivotal to supporting and leading staff in making decisions around data. Typically such teams consisted of the principal, assistant principal, data management support staff (made up of other administrators and teachers), and grade-level representatives. At all school sites, leadership teams were critical to building capacity for facilitating conversations around data as well as translating data into action plans.

The presence of stable, strong, and distributed leadership at both the district and school levels had obvious advantages for the implementation of data use. Leaders were able to lay the groundwork for reform over a period of years rather than having to start reform from the position of being newly appointed in a site. As we will discuss in chapter 4, this helped leaders establish trust and a culture of support for data-informed decision making.

The Policy Context: High-Stakes Accountability

Accountability policies at the state and federal levels loom large in data use efforts, and the sites we studied were no exception. All were located in states with strong accountability systems, state curricular standards linked to state assessments, and consequences for schools not showing improvement over a multiyear period. District and school personnel were keenly aware of the possibility of state sanctions if they did not achieve on the measures set forth by No Child Left Behind (NCLB). Thus, all of the schools and districts felt as though they were under considerable pressure to produce or maintain high levels of achievement.

At one district A school, the threat of being labeled "low performing" by the state initially motivated teachers to become more engaged with standards-based instruction and to start monitoring students' progress toward standards using benchmark assessments that they created themselves. One teacher explained, "It was projected that we were going to be a Program Improvement School because of test scores dipping one year. . . . We got a heads-up that we better do something." The school staff decided to be proactive, as did the district, which began working with external providers to help them improve standards-based education and develop a data management system. The district became one of the early adopters of the system, the school did not fall into Program Improvement status, and student performance increased. Overall, district administrators perceived the accountability policies as a positive turn, despite some concerns about how they held schools responsible for their results. They noted that it was possible for schools merely to chase the numbers without doing what was right for the students; thus, they focused on looking beyond the numbers and decided to use multiple measures of accountability.

State accountability policies also had great deal of influence on the way that district C operated, monitored progress, and assessed performance. The state assessment system predated NCLB and made school data available for public review. In fact, school test results were printed in local newspapers. Initially district C was ranked fifty-second out of fifty-four districts in the state. As a result of the low ranking, the district's board and superintendent team established goals, policies, and a plan of action to improve performance. A district administrator referred to the state accountability system as the "measuring stick that we're judged by." As one site administrator concluded, "Accountability is a strong force for change. It is truly the change agent. More important, if the reliability and the validity of the system you're using are not good, then your change will be flawed." District B had a rigorous data collection and analysis system before the implementation of NCLB; data-informed decision making had been part of the district culture since at least the early 1990s when districtwide assessments were implemented. One change made as a result of NCLB was that the district had to disaggregate data by student demographic subgroups, which it had not done previously.

Clearly all three districts were located in states with strong accountability systems that helped to frame their efforts at data use. This provided political leverage for leaders as it motivated staff to focus on improving student achievement. All three districts were noted as high performing, but all had gone through periods of reform as a result of their disappointment with low student achievement. The context for data-informed decision making would clearly be different in sites with consistently strong records of achievement, or where the relevant policy did not involve high-stakes accountability for student results. As we explain in later chapters, the impetus for using data would have to be different. In fact, these conditions might be quite freeing.

Practices and Patterns: Common Reform Features

By design, each of the districts in our study was a known leader in data use, and the specific school sites we studied were considered to be far along in their efforts to use data. As a result, they shared some common practices and patterns:

- All of the districts had systemwide interim assessments and curricula aligned to state standards, although the schools had some flexibility to make instructional changes based on student needs, particularly if the case could be made using data.

- The school sites had norms and cultures that supported data use, and they had common structures in place to support data use by teachers, partly driven by the larger accountability and reform movements focused on system coherence and alignment.

- Schools administered benchmark assessments quarterly or more frequently, and teachers were asked to examine the results in collaborative groups.

- Leaders strongly encouraged teachers to use a range of assessments of student learning for formative purposes in planning their instruction. They encouraged teachers to think broadly about what constituted data that would inform teaching and learning.

- The districts stored data in Web-based information systems that teachers could access. Such systems enabled users to obtain student achievement and demographic data in a timely and accessible manner. All three districts used staff at the district and school site levels to aid teachers in managing and using the data.

As we flesh out in the next three chapters, the cultures of these schools and districts supported data use reform in almost every way. Leaders took great care to develop trust among teachers, assuage their concerns about how the data reflected on them as individual teachers, and promote a positive orientation toward data use. Most important, these schools and districts were capable reform sites. We chose them for the study because they are leaders in data use and had improved student achievement over time. By and large, positive relationships and practices were already in place before data use was introduced. They were focused on continuous improvement even before data use became a priority. All of these factors made these sites cases of promising practices in data-informed leadership.

In many ways, the districts and schools in our study represent the ideal conditions for data use. Of course it is preferable to have stable, supportive people in leadership positions and practices and patterns that support data use, among other key features. That said, the lessons we outline in this book are useful to educators in a range of contexts because they show the myriad ways in which supports for data use were built. We uncover not only what promising practices were in place, but also how leaders arrived at them. The lessons suggest the benefits when leaders build their own and their staff's skills to use data well by grounding reform efforts in a deep knowledge of the four critical Ps: the people, policies, practices, and patterns that shape their worlds at school or in the district.

To Sum Up

The people, policies, practices, and patterns that comprise a school or district are powerful shaping forces in educational change. Any attempt to introduce data-informed decision making without fully understanding and acknowledging their significance will be fraught with difficulties. Context is everything.

Questions for Discussion

As leaders begin to grapple with the importance of context in their data use efforts, they would be wise to ask themselves the following questions:

- What is the prior reform history? What experiences have teachers had with other initiatives that may be similar to this one?

- How stable is the leadership at the district and school levels? Is leadership spread over multiple individuals at the school level?

- Who are the key people among the teaching staff who will help or hinder data use efforts?

- What is the existing professional capacity of teachers and leaders to undertake new practices?

- What patterns of interaction exist among people that can either facilitate or thwart change?

- What current routines and practices may support data use? And what existing ways of doing things will get in the way?

- How do changing state and federal policies shape data use efforts here? How does the current record of achievement, as measured by accountability systems, shape the potential for data use?

Chapter 3

Reculturing for Data Use

Stony Field, a suburban district whose students have always performed well on standardized tests, presents an example of the challenges of building a culture of productive data use. It has been difficult for district leaders to motivate some teachers to rigorously examine data and their own practices because they believe the current instructional model is working. The district has also faced pressure from parents to maintain high levels of performance. This has made some teachers fearful of trying new approaches because they might lead to a drop in test scores.

Meanwhile, district leaders have grown increasingly concerned that the state test is not measuring the higher-order thinking skills that they hope students will learn. They want teachers to examine evidence on student learning more closely. The district invested in a data management system to enable teachers to use data more efficiently. But teachers, who were accustomed to a high degree of autonomy, questioned why the district wanted to collect the data and how they would be used. They worried they would be so busy grading and entering data that they would not have enough time to prepare for teaching.

Through careful scheduling, teachers at each grade level have at least two hours of collaboration time every week. Although some grade levels make efforts to get together on a regular or semiregular basis, others do not. Maria, a district administrator who has spent many years in the classroom, reflected on the need to shift the culture of teacher meetings from a focus on trivial issues to rigorous inquiry around student work:

In my experience, demystifying what goes on inside the "black box" is rarely done in a systematic way, even between teachers whose classrooms are right next door to one another. We share worksheets and project ideas and may even sit down and plan weekly schedules together, but we don't seem to get the opportunity to observe one another in the classroom, sit down and analyze data, or share responsibility for students who are not meeting proficiency benchmarks.

A culture shift was required in order to create the conditions for this to occur.

———————

Motivating educators to focus on shared accountability for students' progress toward meaningful goals is an important leadership practice, but building such a culture and developing a shared sense of purpose can be a challenge. Educators who are going to use data thoughtfully need to work in a culture that supports data use as a tool for continuous improvement. Building such a culture requires leaders to help staff move beyond accountability data and away from an attitude of simple compliance to external mandates.

Creating a Culture of Data Use for Continuous Improvement

Leadership is about influencing not just practices but also beliefs and norms. As such, leaders play a pivotal role in establishing a data-informed decision-making culture. The leaders in our study understood that they could not simply mandate productive use of data; they also had to work on helping the people in their organizations understand the vision and purpose of data use.

In this chapter, we share lessons from district and school leaders to show how schools and systems can enable productive data use. We explain how system and school leaders worked together to create explicit norms and expectations for continuous improve-ment as they engendered a climate of trust so that teachers could openly discuss data without fear of repercussions. We describe how leaders were able to shift the culture in their schools and dis-tricts to facilitate meaningful data use. This required deliberate effort on the part of leaders to change the culture by promoting new norms, frames, and belief systems. We refer to this as *recul-turing*.[1] To provide research-based lessons for other leaders, we describe the specific actions and activities that we observed lead-ers undertaking at the school and district levels. We explain how they worked collaboratively and individually to accomplish the goal of reculturing, and we also illuminate the challenges they encountered along the way.

In keeping with the model of distributed leadership that we discussed in chapter 1, the process of reculturing at the school and district levels must:

- Be shared and reinforced by leadership teams
- Include strong linkages between district and school leaders
- Frame data use in a way that engenders trust rather than suspicion in the minds of teachers

This last component may be the most difficult, especially in the current policy climate in which teachers are often blamed for the underachievement of their students.

The three districts we studied had to cultivate an interest in data-informed decision making with a wide variety of principals and teachers, many of whom had been in the system for some time. It is important to note that the stability of the leadership in the districts undoubtedly contributed to their ability to engage the trust of principals and teachers in building a culture of data use and establishing a shared sense of responsibility. And as we described in chapter 2, there was also a history of trust between principals and district staff, and this certainly played a role. The districts had similar approaches to cultivating interest at the school level in data-informed practices, and we can learn a great deal from their experiences.

The Role of Culture in Enabling Data Use: Partnerships between Schools and Districts

Earlier studies on data use reveal the importance of focusing on structures as well as directly addressing the school and district culture. We focus on structures in the next chapter and here turn our attention to the centrality of school and district cultures. Prior research makes a compelling case for the key role of district staff in school improvement (and, we would argue, in data use), contending that many past efforts at school reform have failed due to limited central office participation.[2] Districts are key actors in educational reform: they provide instructional leadership, reorient the organization, establish coherence, and maintain an equity focus.[3] Research on districts underscores the importance of open, clear lines of communication between teachers and the district in promoting a professional community that supports instructional reform.[4] These elements are critical in order for a district to realize its goals.

A study of data use efforts in multiple districts found that a trusting data use culture was an important enabler of more complex forms of data-informed decision making.[5] Where trust existed, teachers felt comfortable constructively challenging each other and saw accountability as helpful rather than threatening. But developing such cultures is not easy because teachers sometimes mistrust data.[6] School leaders themselves often have anxiety about their own data literacy and ability to lead in data-informed ways, and this unease can lead to a lack of confidence and a feeling of powerlessness.[7] For many leaders, a fundamental mind shift needs to occur so that data are understood not only as tools for accountability purposes but also as aids in continuous improvement efforts.

Keeping both excellence and equity at the forefront of the school or district agenda is key in creating a culture of data-informed decision making. For example, leaders in some districts that had raised achievement for low-income students and students of color moved their staff to think about students in terms of their assets rather than their deficits, and they focused on ensuring that all children reached high standards.[8] Leaders like these honor diversity, promote dialogue among diverse stakeholders, and have high expectations for all children.[9]

In sum, one of the most important elements in building a culture for data use is fostering a climate of shared responsibility for school improvement between the district and the schools.[10] In fact, this has been identified as a key feature of districts that have successfully supported instructional change. Honig and Copland called such arrangements "learning focused partnerships with schools."[11] Instead of focusing on monitoring and compliance, the district administrators in their study developed partnerships with school leaders that were rooted in notions of reciprocal accountability and the idea that both district offices and schools held important knowledge about improving student learning.

> *One of the most important elements in building a culture for data use is fostering a climate of shared responsibility for school improvement between the district and the schools.*

With this background research in mind, we turn to how the leaders in our study shifted the culture in their contexts.

Understanding How Change Happens and Using Data Thoughtfully

To create a productive culture of data use, leaders must first understand how change occurs, what barriers stand in the way, and how improvement efforts can be sustained. Having an understanding of this necessary precondition, the leaders in our study informed their theory of action about how to implement data use and what types of leadership activities would be needed to get people on board with the reform.

In district A, leaders explicitly talked about their theory of change and the sustainability of reform. They understood that because the use of data for decision making across the system was a new endeavor, they could not simply mandate change or assume that people would automatically see the inherent value of their efforts. The superintendent acknowledged that change, particularly long-term change, takes time:

> You know, you put a new wrapper on the box because it's fun to change the paper, but to really change what's in the box is difficult. And I think that what we've accepted is we've got to get to the difficult work, which is changing our behaviors. And that takes time.

In spite of their long-term ambitions for data use and educational reform, district leaders were mindful that change had to happen slowly and incrementally. As the superintendent explained, "We're just on the verge of what we could do, but you can't create such angst among adults. You've got to always be strategic about 'how far can I push before I push them over the edge?'"

In any reform implementation, leaders must consider the emotional reactions and cognitive demands they are asking educators to take on. Those who participated in our study understood that. Furthermore, the district administrators in district A believed strongly in data-informed decision making, but made a point to say how important it was to use data properly and thoughtfully. Reflecting on their use of data to improve the placement and scheduling of students, the superintendent said, "So that's the big message in data: it's only good if you think real carefully about what you are trying to achieve."

A school administrator in district C similarly argued that data were important because they helped educators pinpoint root causes of problems. She cautioned her colleagues, however, that data lead only to questions; solutions then emerge by analyzing root causes. She used a medical analogy:

> I can give you an aspirin if you have a headache. But if your head hurts because you've had an aneurysm, then giving you aspirin isn't going to help. It's the same thing with education and data. If you don't examine the data and look deeply at the root causes, you might just be solving the wrong problem or addressing the problem the wrong way. And in the end, that won't help the students.

District administrators hoped that teachers would learn to use data in ways that did not create more work but instead helped them to "work smarter." Rather than leading to the general identification of standards or areas that students were struggling with, the hope was that data would help teachers dig deeper into root causes. For example, rather than identifying that a particular student was struggling with phonemic awareness, data could be used to pinpoint the exact area of difficulty—perhaps breaking down multisyllabic words. For the leaders in both districts A and C, data helped to start the inquiry process of understanding how to improve teaching and learning.

All of the sites in our study shared one important component of a culture of data-informed decision making: support from the principal. Paralleling the district's message about using data thoughtfully, the principal of one high school in district A worked hard to support the culture of data use. A teacher told us that the principal made clear that data use was a focus at the school even before she hired her: "It was really something that [the principal] wanted to push. . . . It's just assumed that you will use the data to help drive what you need to do and where you need to go." The principal was credited by another teacher as presenting data use in "a positive light." The teacher went on to explain that the principal did so by treating it also as a learning opportunity that was scaffolded: "I mean she's offered opportunities that if you struggle, here's your safety net. If you've failed, try again. You know she's done it in a very nonjudgmental way and let people get to their levels." The principal's attitude and working relationship with staff on data use reflected the district's emphasis on building capacity. When leaders take this approach, they acknowledge that different people are at different levels of development with a new practice and thus may require different types of support.

Establishing Expectations

Data-informed leaders play a critical role in creating explicit expectations to combat negative perceptions and taken-for-granted assumptions about data use that could create barriers. In part this means that schools and districts must make it the norm to base decisions on evidence, and they must also engender an inquiry-minded culture at the teacher team, school, and district levels. Schools and central offices collaborated closely in order to make improvements. Districts emphasized the need for mutual accountability and schools were held accountable for results, but the main responsibility of the central office was to support schools and provide resources. The schools and districts had trusting relationships with two-way communication flows. Importantly, principals in all three districts indicated that they had supportive relationships with administrators in the central office.

Over time, district C leaders developed firm expectations that every decision would be supported by data. Many staff members echoed one district administrator who said, "We don't do anything without the data. You can't make a good decision without data because if you do, then it's just a hunch or just a guess." District C leaders set an expectation that principals should not ask for additional resources or staff without using data as supporting evidence. But these high expectations were a two-way street, and teachers and principals were encouraged to view the district as a support provider and partner in their efforts. One principal in district C explained: "The district does an exceptional job of training us, of communicating with us, helping us with data and how to interpret it."

District B expected everyone to use data and, as one teacher put it, to "not fumble around in the dark" or, as another joked, to avoid "shooting darts blindfolded." Accordingly, the district provided quick access to data. A teacher explained: "We're in lockstep. The district believes in data, the principal believes in data, and we believe in data. I mean, there's really no other way to go." Teachers noted that data "open your eyes more" and help educators realize that teaching doesn't always lead to learning. For example, a math teacher may have covered long division in class, but if the majority of students fail to understand how to solve problems on their own, then the teaching did not lead to student learning. Data also provided opportunities to see and celebrate incremental successes.

In order to foster a culture conducive to data use, district A presented data as a necessary tool for practice. The assistant superintendent explained, "We have to instill in our teachers the desire that other professionals have, whether they're medical professionals or other things, that they can't imagine doing their job without having data, to be held accountable but not given any tools to get there. . . . It just needs to be an expectation, like health benefits and a decent salary; they ought to expect those tools."

For data to be truly useful, educators need to follow through and take actions based on their understanding of the information, and not just have a culture that promotes the use of data. The superintendent of district A asked:

> *What good are data if they don't change something? It is like knowing your blood pressure is high, but if you don't do anything about it, you're going to die anyway. Well, you might as well stop taking the reading!*

Thus, district leaders imbued school staff with autonomy to make decisions on the basis of data, especially with regard to within-school and after-school interventions for low-performing students. For example, the district A principal explained, "Every year [the intervention classes] looked different, and it still looks different. Every year we analyze the data on our intervention and have been willing to tweak it, even though it drives us crazy." The district also believed strongly in the power of teacher leadership and capacity building among teachers. As the superintendent explained, "Principals come and go. Superintendents come and go. The only way you're really going to change our system is when you change the belief of the people doing the work in it." With these ideas in mind, district A worked to build a culture of commitment, rather than compliance, among all of their teachers.

Sharing Data for Decision Making

Cultural change was sometimes slow to develop. In district A, it began to take hold through a series of interrelated steps. In their effort to build a culture that modeled data sharing and use at the highest level of leadership first, the district examined the district-wide data as a whole. They then produced school-level reports in which each school was compared to the rest of the district and, in turn, centered data examination at individual school sites so that administrators and teachers could reflect on the strengths and weaknesses of their own schools. District leaders facilitated the sharing of school-level data among the schools and ensured that teachers had access to their own class data. Principals and data teams had access to all of the teachers' data at each school site.

Collaboration was highly valued across all sites as the basis for sharing data. However, collaboration did not mean that conflict or disagreements did not happen. In fact, healthy debates were more likely to occur when trust already existed and working together toward a common goal was the norm. A principal in district C remarked that the key to making data relevant was the working relationships that developed between staff because, she said, "without collaboration and the collegiality, data [use] is impossible." She acknowledged that staff members had "lively discussions" and recalled one incident where teachers in one department argued that assessing students every week was too often. She acknowledged that "we fought, we fought, we fought," and eventually they resolved the issue through multiple discussions about the relevance of data and the need for frequent testing. One school administrator had the slogan, "Whatever happens in your meeting, stays in your meeting." Her philosophy was that disagreements should occur because "if you don't disagree, then there's something wrong because you've got ten different personalities."

> Healthy debates were more likely to occur when trust already existed and working together toward a common goal was the norm.

Similarly, in district B, both the principal and the district leaders tried to create a "we feeling" with respect to student results. The principal worked to cultivate a team spirit in examining data: "One of my big things is that we're all responsible for all of the data that come back. Just because it's an English score doesn't mean we can't all be helping." She worked explicitly on helping all staff feel responsible for data results regardless of the department or content area. The goal was to create a sense of how they could work together to use or improve an area rather than asking, "Whose fault is this?" Promoting this norm also fit with the district's and school's belief in the importance of collaboration and collegiality.

This attitude existed in at least one of the local school sites in district B; we saw similar patterns at the high school we studied. A teacher captured this poignantly:

> Some teachers do not like getting bad data back. For me, if I get bad data back, I wonder, "What am I doing wrong, and what do I need to fix?" Some people think, "Oh, I'm a bad teacher." They just do that emotional shutdown. I think when our team gets back bad data they think, "Oh no, these data are awful. What are you doing?" They automatically ask, "What are you doing that's right, and let's do that."

As his comment suggests, some teacher teams developed cultures in which data could be assessed in a nonjudgmental way, whereas in others, teachers found the process more personally difficult. (We take up the issue of teacher collaboration dynamics in more detail in chapters 4 and 5.)

As much as district and school leaders emphasized viewing data objectively and in a nonpersonalized way, this wasn't always an appropriate approach. After all, teachers were reflecting on data that potentially had consequences for students' academic trajectories and lives. Several teachers admitted that it was difficult not to take the data personally because they were so invested in their students. The data also informed their own judgments of professional competence and sense of efficacy. Therefore, taking a completely nonemotional stance wasn't always possible, and it was not always reasonable.

Building Trust through Flexibility and Teacher Expertise

The creation of trust in data use requires an approach that respects all of the people involved and is flexible enough to make sense within specific schools and classrooms. Districts A and C began their data use efforts in the past decade, but data-informed decision making has been part of the district culture in district B since the early 1990s when districtwide assessments were implemented. Using the image of a triangle with curriculum, instruction, and assessment as the key components, district B administrators promoted the idea of continual data-informed adjustments in alignment with the sides of the triangle. They believed that:

- Teachers were experts in curriculum, instruction, and assessment.
- Data were critical to finding out whether teachers were succeeding in delivering curriculum-guided instruction.
- Assessments should be relevant to daily teaching practice.

They therefore had teachers write the assessments themselves and grade them using common rubrics. Teacher input continually informed each dimension of the triangle. By promoting teacher engagement, district B built a culture for data use.

District B schools were given flexibility and district-level support, but they were also held to high expectations. The district set the tone regarding the alignment of curriculum, instruction, and assessment, and schools were expected to follow through with implementation. Although some decisions were made collaboratively, there was also a sense of a tightly coupled hierarchy regarding information distribution and policy implementation. In spite of this, there was a collaborative attitude at the district and school levels that led to good communication. It was not uncommon for teachers in various departments to call colleagues at other schools if they needed assistance teaching particular lessons.

Teachers cannot effectively use data if they worry that the data might be used punitively against them. To address this issue, the administrators in district A worked hard to build trusting relationships with school site administrators and teachers and to create a nonthreatening atmosphere of data use. They were clear that teachers would not be evaluated or penalized for their students' performance on assessment; rather, the goal was for teachers to use the data as tools for seeing where teaching and learning growth or change were needed.

Some teachers at the high school in district A remarked specifically on the high degree of trust the principal had in the teachers and how clear it was that she respected their judgment. The principal even allowed teachers to opt out of a districtwide professional development because apparently the teachers were more knowledgeable than the instructor. "My point is that we have a lot of say," said one teacher. Another reported that she believed she had the flexibility to make changes in her classroom on the basis of data because the principal "lets me know she's very confident in what I do in class."

Establishing the routine of data use must be approached with care and thought. A principal in district A explained that when she initially came to her site, she had to present the use of data in a positive manner so that teachers understood that she was not trying to single out or criticize people. People were defensive when confronted with data, and so she began framing the data as an indicator of how the school *as a team* needed to improve. Another principal initially tried to make data use more palatable to teachers by consistently reminding them that the data would be used for asking questions and helping to make improvements. She noted that when a teacher expressed sentiments such as, "This is so depressing. I worked so hard, and these are my scores," she responded, "Don't go there. Don't look at it that way. What we need to do then is to say, 'Okay, what can we do differently next time?'" Such a culture took time to develop, and teachers at this site reported that they had to undergo a paradigm shift regarding the purposes of student achievement data. When they stopped viewing data as highlighting "what I can't do," they began to see it the data as "what I need help on."

Some of the lead teachers we interviewed echoed the district's doctor/lab results analogy, expressing comfort with the idea that data were diagnostic tools rather than an evaluation of their abilities. One teacher compared their situation to a dentist's: "The dentist works on a patient's teeth and gets the best results that are possible. You don't hear the dentist say, 'My patient has a new cavity, but I filled three last year, so I must not be a good dentist.'" Although medical analogies have obvious limitations, they served to depersonalize the process of looking at data.

In district C, there was general consensus that data use was a powerful tool for school improvement, although gaining buy-in to this idea initially posed various challenges. The superintendent remembered that in the beginning, the principals did not believe that the district's benchmark assessments were valid. She recalled, "It took about three years to make believers out of our principals" before they acknowledged the validity of the district-developed benchmark assessments. Teachers provided input into the development of the benchmark assessments as well.

Much as in district A, district C administrators worked on developing a culture where data could be discussed without fear of repercussions. The superintendent explained that staff members needed to "trust that their world would not end if their data were bad or if they made a bad decision." She noted that if data showed poor student performance, the information was framed in a way that acknowledged that instructional strategies for groups or specific students were not effective, rather than as, "Gotcha! You're doing a poor job." She believed that developing a sense of trust was a "top-down, bottom-up, side-by-side" process, with the goal that principals and teachers would feel comfortable coming to meetings to share data. This again was a reflection of the district's desire to build a culture focused on continuous improvement, where mistakes were used as opportunities for improvement. This type of orientation also provided space for principals and teachers to innovate and try new practices.

Creating a Culture of High Expectations for Student Learning

Data can be powerful in helping to build a culture of ownership

> *Data can be powerful in helping to build a culture of ownership for improving achievement for all students.*

for improving achievement for all students. We found this in numerous sites we studied. And at both the district and school levels, building a culture for data use can involve creating a situation in which discussions of students' abilities are focused not on deficits but on existing student strengths and how they can be expanded.

All of the sites we studied were serving large numbers of low-income students of color. Addressing teachers' low expectations for students who have come from underprivileged backgrounds was a hurdle that had to be initially overcome in some of them. For example, a principal in district A explicitly persuaded her staff: "Yes, we have challenges, but our kids can do it. Now, look at other schools that are doing it, and comparing them, we can do it." She noted that the shift toward understanding the relevance of data did not come about until the school began to disaggregate data at the teacher level. Specifically, teachers began to shift their beliefs about students when the school as a whole started to examine individual teacher data for their students, teacher attendance, and so forth. Teachers began to examine their own specific strengths and weaknesses, and conversations shifted toward how they could help each other improve their practices.

The accountability system can compel teachers and schools to examine how they are serving all students and not just those who were able to learn "in spite of what we do." The mandate to disaggregate student data by subgroups allowed district C to point to achievement differences among student groups and create a call to action among teachers. A district administrator explained that the district's goal became to narrow the performance gap among all subgroups, and particularly between students of color and white students. She attributed the district's success to the beliefs that they had engendered about their students: "There's ownership for every student. We take them where they are, regardless, and we move them as far and as quickly as we can. When they walk in the door, they belong to us."

The development of this belief system took time. The superintendent believed that once teachers could say that instructional strategies, not the children, were the problem, then learning could happen for every child. She argued, "Until you change the philosophy of the teacher, nothing will make a big difference." She believed that the first step in the challenging task of changing attitudes was building trust so that teachers felt secure enough to come to a meeting and say, "My kids are not learning," and then ask, "How can you help me?" Slowly this culture filtered through the school sites.

District A also attempted to cultivate a climate of high expectations, and data were integral to this process. A data team leader at one school said, "A huge part of our vision is to just never get complacent about who our kids are and to never make assumptions about them either." The majority of staff members we interviewed expressed positive beliefs about their students' abilities to meet high expectations. One of the fifth-grade teachers simply said, "We don't just say, 'Well this group can't do it.' That isn't the language here." Another teacher added that the school's philosophy was not, "'That child can't do it,' but, 'What do we have to do to make sure they can do it?'" Similarly, in district B, there was a strong sense among school and district personnel that all students could learn and should be held to high standards. One teacher enthusiastically reported the attitude that teachers had toward student learning: "The teachers at this school think that they can get anybody to pass anything."

Data can be integral to changing old mind-sets. In district A, district leaders presented data to elementary school principals and teachers to make a case for raising expectations:

> We showed them that if students don't leave sixth grade proficient or advanced [on the state tests], the likelihood that they are going to get into ninth grade and be successful in rigorous college prep classes is greatly reduced. Furthermore, if they leave you below or far below basic, the likelihood that they even graduate gets slimmer and slimmer. Teachers are going, "Boy, this isn't okay. We've got to do this." We'll see what happens, but that was one of the strongest motivators that I've seen with our teachers. And it was just simple—the same little charts we used with the high school folks.

District A leaders focused on more than numerical data. They also relied on observational data of students and classrooms. "It gives you a bird's-eye view of your system that's kind of painful to see, but you can't fix it if you don't look at it," explained the superintendent. We explain how the district used observational data in more detail in chapter 5.

Shifts in Beliefs and Ongoing Tensions

In spite of challenges at the beginning, teachers across the study sites came to view data as relevant and necessary. One teacher said data helped her to reflect on her instruction and made her realize that in order to improve student learning, "It's not acceptable to just stand up and teach, because [students] are not getting it. I need to look at what other strategies I can use." Many teachers across the three districts noted how data revealed disparities between what they taught and what the students actually learned and also helped assess not only students' strengths but their weaknesses in learning.

Examining data can shed light on problems that have previously been ignored, especially for certain groups of students. For example, in one school, the teachers realized that the scores of about 45 percent of the advanced-level students had fallen in a single year. This information helped them to realize that rather than focusing only on struggling students, they also needed to challenge the more advanced students. In some ways, data were used to confirm what teachers formerly might have known based on professional judgment. A district administrator likened this to watching one's weight: "I don't have to step on a scale to know that my clothes don't feel right."

Most staff members, and leaders in particular, were able to express why and how data were pivotal to making instructional changes. Many staff members remarked that data were a powerful tool to identify one's areas of strengths and weaknesses in order to make improvements. Teachers remarked that data provided "a focus and direction" for their instruction. One teacher who had been at a school for over a decade believed that the use of data had made an important difference because, she said, "Back in the day, you could do what you felt like doing, plus you enjoyed doing it, but that's not necessarily what the child needed." A teacher in district B expressed similar ideas, emphasizing the importance of data for sound decision making: "I think you have to use data or else you won't know how you're doing and then you can't get better. How are you going to get better if you don't know how you did?" Another stated, "It helps me make more professional decisions about where I want to take my students." In other words, using data gave teachers more focus and contributed to developing shared understandings of problems and solutions.

There were, of course, varied opinions among teachers, which led to critical and healthy conversations about the use of data in schools. Most of the critiques revolved around what educators perceived as a narrow window offered by the data. One teacher in district B said, "I'm a true believer that data do show a little bit but don't show the whole story." Similarly, teachers in district A found assessment data useful for improving instruction, but some acknowledged they did not tell everything they needed to know to help students be successful: the data could help pinpoint problems but couldn't tell the teachers exactly how to improve their practice. In addition, one teacher noted that some students did not take the tests seriously, so the scores were not a true reflection of their achievement: "There are kids that actually take it seriously and do well. But for a lot of these kids, there's no buy-in for them to take it seriously, and they know that." Another teacher noted that an additional potential area of trouble was the assessments themselves. She asked, "Was it even a good test question? It helps us then re-create tests or look at the test and say, 'That's a good one,' or 'That doesn't ask anything that we've been teaching.'"

Undoubtedly, school cultures are difficult to change, a finding that is supported by decades of research.[12] The examples we have shared here show the achievements and challenges that schools have faced in trying to establish cultures where making decisions based on data becomes a taken-for-granted feature of school life. Disaggregating the data by race, ethnicity, and income status and looking at multiple measures of student achievement provided the occasion to confront issues and reshape expectations for students. As part of this process, school and district leaders have attempted to create a culture of high expectations for all students. The efforts we observed in schools and districts to use data to change the dialogue around equity are supported by the research. Most districts are evolving from their tolerance for a wide range of outcomes among students, and it is no longer acceptable to district leaders, the state, or the public that only a small proportion of students in a school system are successful.[13] Thus, what we are arguing for here is not entirely new, but its importance needs to be underscored.

At the same time, effective school districts recognize that equitable outcomes for students are not necessarily achieved by dividing resources equally. Rather, such districts have a "do what it takes" attitude to ensure that all students are given the resources and opportunities they need to be successful. This often results in targeting support to programs for students who have the greatest needs. Numerous districts have been documented as providing "just-in-time" support for students facing academic difficulty so that they do not fall far behind. Principals and teachers in these districts were encouraged to use benchmark assessment data to identify students in need of assistance.[14]

To Sum Up

While all of the districts and schools in our study dealt with multiple challenges with regard to gaining support from staff, they were successful at creating cultures of data use focused on continuous improvement. Creating and maintaining this type of culture required ongoing effort from all of the districts, especially as leadership changes occurred, new policies arose, and new teachers were hired. All were clear that reliance on data-informed decision making had become ingrained in daily organizational life. We must remember that such cultures for data use are not present in many places, and developing them takes substantial, deliberate effort on the part of leaders at all levels.

Questions for Discussion

The following discussion questions for leaders arise from the lessons included in this chapter:

- What is the existing culture regarding educational change? Do educators approach change with a sense of excitement, trepidation, fear, or all of these?

- Which of the explicit expectations and norms described in this chapter can be used to help set the stage for building a data-informed model of continuous improvement?

- How can data-informed leaders in the system model thoughtful data use?

- Does a culture of mutual accountability currently exist among teachers, principals, and district personnel? If not, which of the lessons in this chapter may be useful in engendering it?

- What data can be brought to bear by principals or district leaders to show the relevance of using data to systematically improve student achievement?

- What data can be analyzed to expose patterns of differential achievement based on student demographic subgroups, confront school and classroom conditions that lead to these patterns, and set high expectations for improving achievement across all groups?

Chapter 4

Goals, Routines, and Tools for Data Use

J ane, a middle school teacher, was on board with data-informed decision making, but she felt the main barrier to data use at her school was the curriculum pacing pressure. The district had adopted a new math curriculum, and district curriculum leaders designed a pacing guide in which textbook lessons were mapped each week throughout the school year. The pace required every math teacher to dedicate approximately one day to teaching each concept. The pacing guide was accompanied by district-mandated benchmark assessments. Jane explained the dilemmas that this produced:

> There are precise dates when every sixth-grade math teacher is required to administer these assessments. My colleagues regularly comment on needing to continue moving forward to be on pace with the benchmark assessments. Interestingly, once administered, results appear not to get reported back to the school sites. More interestingly, when I brought this up at a team meeting, no one else had noticed the lack of feedback or seemed to desire to get the data back. Finally, the year-end state test exerts a pacing pressure of its own as the test is administered mid-April, two months before the end of the school year, and assesses all content standards expected to be taught by the end of the school year.

She explained that using the data to inform targeted, individualized instruction "would certainly interfere with the fast pace of curricular coverage." When she asked her colleagues how they responded to students who did not understand particular lessons, they often said, "There is no time to wait; just keep moving."

Jane was understandably frustrated that the pacing plan got in the way of her genuine interest in gearing instruction around students' individual needs. She saw it as a "racing guide" rather than a pacing guide. Clearly, the benchmark assessments her district administered were not facilitating the process of data-informed instruction.

Organizational goals, routines, and tools structure work inside schools. At times, they can serve to maintain the status quo, especially when they are driven by the mantra, "That's how we've always done things here." But new elements can bring change and help to transform practices; when this happens, organizational goals, routines, and tools can facilitate data use if they are used effectively and carefully considered. In this way, old habits can be questioned and new ones can emerge. By focusing on these aspects, we can see what changes in practice and what stays the same.[1] We can pay attention to the interactions that take place among people engaged in activities rather than attributing all change to the actions of a leader. Because we recognize that leadership is present in many places, not just in formally appointed individuals such as the principal or the superintendent, this focus on routines that involve a broader range of educators makes sense.

Let's begin by examining a few of the common tools and routines that are meant to facilitate the process of data use:

- *Common curricular guidelines:* Many leaders point to the value of common curricular guidelines because they allow teachers to jointly plan and have discussions about student data; they can provide teachers with an opportunity to situate their problems of practice on common ground and can facilitate the assessment of students' progress toward an agreed-on set of standards.[2] In the United States, where states are required to have curriculum standards for every grade level and subject, districts have typically created a set of structural supports to provide teachers with guidance on curricular units, materials, and lesson planning. Districts vary in the flexibility they allow teachers in terms of staying on a strict district curricular pacing plan or allowing site and classroom-level flexibility around a set of standards. This level of flexibility turns out to be very important. As we saw in the example at the start of this chapter, such plans can help teachers come to shared understandings and agreements about goals and actions. Districts across the United States are working to revamp these support structures with the implementation of the Common Core Standards, but pacing plans that are too strict can inhibit data-informed instruction.

• *Benchmark assessments:* Many districts also use benchmark assessments as a key feature of their data use efforts. The tests, typically administered every six to twelve weeks, are intended to serve as guideposts for future instruction and as indications of student progress toward state standards.[3] Typically these benchmark assessments are aligned to annual state assessment tests. Many districts purchased their assessments, and some of these have item banks that district staff or teachers can select from. In other cases, districts create their own benchmark assessments. The intent of these assessments is to give district and school leaders, as well as individual teachers, a sense of how students are progressing toward the standards throughout the year and how well they are being prepared, especially for the year-end high-stakes accountability tests. Teachers can examine the data and make midcourse adjustments to their instruction. Many districts have invested in data management systems through which the results of benchmark assessments are made available, and these systems are another important tool in the data use process. New benchmark assessments are being developed to align to the Common Core Standards in the United States.

• *Structured teacher collaboration:* To enable teachers to plan instruction together and discuss assessment results, many districts have established time for structured teacher collaboration.[4] The belief is that by working together, teachers will be able to assist each other in making sense of the data, engage in joint action planning, and share instructional strategies. The presence of a leader who promotes a culture of inquiry in a teacher work group can also aid in making conversations productive.[5] Teacher collaboration is believed to be an essential ingredient of any school improvement effort. However, it does not automatically lead to improved teaching and learning or to teacher reflection.[6] A great deal depends on the inquiry that occurs in these groups, and certain conditions can be counterproductive to data use. For example, the knowledge of data use within and among teacher groups can vary widely, leading to uneven results in the analysis of data. Teacher teams with limited expertise can misinterpret or misuse data, or when they work together, they might perpetuate poor classroom practice.[7] Groups with a great deal of collective expertise can generate much more learning.[8] Similarly, many districts have rushed to implement benchmark assessments without fully thinking through the conditions that would enable them to be used effectively.

Presumably we have well-intentioned district and school leaders who aim to improve student achievement and wish to support teachers' use of data through the implementation of curricular plans and useful benchmark assessments. But how might data-informed leaders avoid these types of land mines? A close examination of the tools, routines, and goals of the three high-performing data use districts we studied provides some important insights. As we will discuss, the establishment of these resources to support data use must happen carefully. We know that if they are seen as top-down initiatives that don't cohere with teachers' daily work, they will not inspire teacher engagement. We begin our discussion with goal setting, an important first step for the data-informed leader.

The Importance of Goal Setting to Measure Progress

Goals for student achievement are an important component of any reform effort, yet often we do not pay enough attention to them. Goal setting is critical not just for data-informed decision making; it is also essential to a cycle of continuous improvement. On one level, the process is quite simple: start with a goal, gather data to see if students have met that goal, analyze the data, and plan your actions accordingly. While this process seems quite straightforward—and it can be—an important precursor is developing the goals themselves. And at that stage, it is important to ask: Who is at the table? How are the goals developed? Are the goals measurable?

Goals for student achievement can be very specific and measurable. Both districts A and C had developed goals connected to their states' accountability systems. For example, district C had a goal that 90 percent of students would meet state standards, 85 percent of students would pass all state tests, and there would be no more than a 3 percent gap between the achievement scores of any two student subgroups. The schools we studied in both districts saw these goals as more of a minimum than an ideal. Each campus in these districts also had its own specific goals beyond student achievement. For example, one school's student behavior goal was to have fewer than 4 percent of their students referred to the office and no suspensions. Data regarding these goals were disaggregated by student subgroup and grade level and updated every six weeks. Students at another school were expected to know daily objectives for the classrooms. In math, for example, when students walked in the classroom door, the principal's expectation was that the class agenda and learning objectives for the day were listed on the board. For example, it might say, "We're going to cover Newton's laws of motion today, and, when you leave, it is your responsibility to apply the first law of motion."

Teachers may also develop their own goals that illustrate their heightened awareness of their students' needs and abilities. One teacher said that although she would like all of her students to achieve at the 90 percent level or above, she set realistic and progressive goals for individual students so that they could celebrate small gains. Some teachers also acknowledged the importance of developing both academic and social skills; they described goals for students to be "well rounded" and to develop interpersonal and speaking skills. They also believed that fostering positive rapport with students and establishing a positive learning environment were important aims.

Administrators in district C distinguished between trailing data—"older data," such as the previous year's state test results—and leading data, from assessments like district benchmarks that are administered more frequently. Previously, state-mandated district and school improvement plans typically had been written but then shelved, but district C had replaced this with a process where trailing data were used to write an action plan and leading data were then used to revise it. As a result, each campus in district C had an action plan that detailed its goals and data as evidence of progress.

A district administrator referred to the action plan as "a living, working document" that was constantly revised and updated based on day-to-day and week-to-week data gathered and examined by the school site. The district did not want a "beautiful pristine document." They preferred to see that data were being used to make changes to the scope and sequence for a six-week period or that a schedule had been rearranged. In our interviews, teachers and administrators handed us packets or binders containing planning documents and data. In one case, the individual apologized for giving us an outdated copy, saying, "This is my plan from a couple of weeks ago." She gestured to another copy with handwritten notes and said, "This is actually my alternate, adjusted action plan." The action plans were created using a template provided by the district that included categories such as objectives, goals, action and tasks, target students, staff responsibilities, measures of success, resource allocation, and scheduled dates for action.

District C also asked school principals to set goals and monitor progress toward them using a scorecard, a districtwide tool that was updated every six weeks. Scorecards were typically compiled by administrators and teachers at each site and reported to area superintendents. They showed student achievement by subject, and they listed growth targets and actual growth in percentages. The reports also included differences between target and actual scores.

With the state's accountability system as leverage for change, district A also began to assess its strengths and weaknesses with regard to student achievement and set goals accordingly. The first strategy was to ensure that curriculum and instruction were aligned to state standards. The district's administrative team then began the next hurdle: establishing meaningful, measurable goals. During this process, they came to the realization that the team was ill equipped to write strong goals by themselves, so they enlisted the aid of a consultant. With the consultant's help, the district leadership underwent a multiyear process of developing and refining their goals, in part by looking closely at past performance data. In the process, they discussed what the superintendent described as "the big challenge": the groups of students whose needs were not being met by the district.

Criteria for the goals were set, including that they be meaningful and measurable at all levels: student, classroom, school, and district. They avoided generalized objectives, such as, "All students become lifelong learners," because they could not be measured. Site administrators and teachers from schools at all levels of the district were part of the final development and refinement process. After three years,

All school staff members we interviewed were able to clearly articulate the district goals, evidence of this district's ability to maintain focus.

the goals were finalized and could be shared throughout the district. The two main goals specified annual progress on the state assessment level and noted that all students would score in the "proficient or above" range within two years. It is noteworthy that all school staff members we interviewed were able to clearly articulate the district goals, evidence of this district's ability to maintain focus.

In some cases, goals may be intentionally vague. District B, for example, did not have specific systemwide goals for student achievement. In the words of the superintendent, "Our goal is: Better tomorrow than we are today. It sounds cliché, but that's about as straightforward as I can make it." The district was held accountable by the state for specific student outcomes on standards-based assessments, and they continually sought to improve student achievement on those measures. Thus, although they did not have measurable districtwide goals, they did have a host of assessments in place and asked teachers at the grade and department levels to establish goals for improving student achievement. Each curricular team created a performance improvement plan that targeted specific goals for improvement throughout the year. The school principal met with each curricular team and asked them specific questions about their plans for improvement, and the plans were revisited at the beginning of the second semester of each year. The prior year's plan helped inform the team of their progress and areas that still needed to be targeted.

Clearly articulated goals helped administrators and teachers monitor student progress regularly and chart action plans accordingly. Districts A and C established goals linked to state tests—an inevitable reality in the No Child Left Behind era in the United States—but goals for students were not limited to performance on state assessments or even limited to academics. Regardless of how goals were defined, a key component was the measurement of progress toward them. Up and down the system, educators were held accountable for continually monitoring whether goals had been

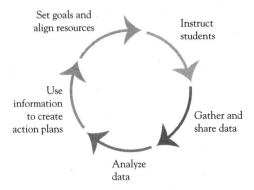

Figure 4.1.   The Cycle of Instructional Improvement
Source: New Schools Venture Fund, *Cycle of Instructional Improvement: Self-Assessment Tool* (San Francisco: New Schools Venture Fund, 2006), http://www.newschools.org/publications/cycle-of-instructional-improvement-tool. Reprinted with permission by New Schools Venture Fund.

reached and what actions might be needed to ensure progress. This process was an integral component of data-informed decision making, and it is part of the cycle of instructional improvement.

The cycle shown in figure 4.1 is helpful in identifying the main processes in data use, but it does not elucidate the critical details within and between stages. During the time between when goals are set and when students are instructed, for example, a host of activities occurs within districts and schools and among the teachers. Some of these activities can be aided by specific tools and routines. We now investigate those further.

Tools: District Curricular Guidelines

Many districts in the United States established districtwide curricular guidelines, most often linked to state standards, and teachers have varying levels of flexibility with how they apply these standards. In some districts, administrators expect to walk into classrooms at a specific grade level and find all teachers working on the same lesson, sometimes even at the same time of day.

Others expect that all areas will be covered but give teachers latitude to use their professional judgment about the pace at which they teach the curriculum. In our study sites, we found that flexibility was important because it gave teachers the ability to adjust their instruction on the basis of data. Without room in their instructional calendars, they had little time to go into more depth in particular topic areas when students needed it or to reteach concepts that some students did not grasp.

Each of the three districts we studied found their districtwide curriculum to be a critical tool in data use. The districts varied in how much flexibility they provided teachers, but all provided some (see table 4.1).

Common Curriculum

A common curriculum ensures that students across classrooms and schools are receiving the same instructional content. In district B, teachers had a common curriculum but were given the freedom to implement it as they saw fit. They had a lot of room to make the decisions that they saw as necessary for their students. However, they were required to attend regular meetings that addressed curricular pacing. Curriculum coordinators worked closely with department chairs and lead mentors in order to

Table 4.1. Levels of Variation in Curricular Flexibility and Pacing Plan by District

	Districtwide Curriculum	Level of Flexibility	Pacing Plan
District A	Yes	Low/middle[a]	Yes
District B	Yes	High	Yes
District C	Yes	High	No

[a]Some teachers perceived the plan as flexible, whereas others did not—hence, the mixed rating.

ensure that curriculum, instruction, and assessment were aligned. Teachers played key roles in developing and maintaining the balance between these three components.

In order to facilitate intradistrict collaboration, the district server contained a bank of lesson plans that district teachers created for each subject. The lesson plan bank encouraged teachers to use the expertise that already existed within the district. There were also districtwide workshops for teachers who taught the same content. At the department or grade level, teacher teams were given the freedom to try various research-based improvements to the curriculum in order to raise scores. This reflected the district administration's belief that teachers would learn and perform better if they had the freedom and support to work together and come up with local solutions.

At the high school level, each department laid out a curriculum map at the beginning of the year noting what would be taught each month. The school we studied had maps across content areas by grade level, and the principal planned to use these maps to look at curricular intersections in order to implement cross-disciplinary curricula. There was a districtwide plan, but the principal wanted teachers at the high school to create their own plans. One teacher described how the department planned for specific development of student skills across the four years of English courses:

> Each level builds upon the last level. We look at the state curriculum but we develop our own curriculum and match it. Everything [is] kind of just building blocks based on what the state tells us we need to do. Sophomore is building on freshman but taking it further. . . . Freshmen start out with expository essays but ultimately by their senior year they're doing the full-blown, five-paragraph literary analysis essay. So each year it's just consecutively building on the last.

District flexibility meant that departments were free to determine the level of standardization to which teachers would subscribe, and we found that they varied quite a bit. The mathematics department in the high school we studied demonstrated the highest level of standardization, whereas the social studies department left the instructional activities very flexible for teachers—in fact, they sometimes had difficulty agreeing with each other on how to teach their course content.

Pacing Plans

A common curriculum dictates what is taught but typically does not inform the pace or depth at which the content is taught. Districts B and C had districtwide curricular guidelines, but district B also had a pacing plan. The district developed these tools over fifteen years ago, well before they invested in data use, due to high student mobility within the district. As students moved from school to school, the district wanted to ensure more seamless transitions with respect to teaching and learning. A district administrator explained that the districtwide curriculum was framed as, "You're going to follow it, and it's nonnegotiable." Based on the state standards, the district's curriculum plan was divided into six-week periods. One school we studied went a step further and broke the six-week sequence and pacing into weekly increments.

District C administrators gave teachers flexibility in how they taught the curriculum. As one district administrator explained it, "The text does not drive the curriculum and you're not going to walk in and find everybody using the same things in the book at the same time." A teacher described the textbooks as "just one of the resources that we use." Another explained, "[The district] gives us lesson plans, but they don't tell us how to teach it." The district C teachers enjoyed this flexibility and the knowledge that supports for teaching the curriculum were available if they needed them. Still, some teachers found the guidelines a bit too constraining. One lead teacher believed that curricular and instructional alignment could be positive for new and "lower-performing teachers, but sometimes the higher-performing teachers almost feel hamstrung by it." He would have liked to devote an entire semester to student-led inquiry for science, but this would have been difficult with the district's guidelines and pacing.

In contrast to the relative flexibility in districts B and C, district A was more strict about adherence to its curriculum pacing plan, and this was met with mixed reviews from the teachers. On the positive side, some believed that curricular coherence across the district was a benefit: "It makes it very nice because if we have kids switching in and out [of different schools within the district] they're all pretty much on the same page." Nevertheless, much like we saw in Jane's case presented at the beginning of the chapter, some teachers felt that the pacing plan in district A did not allow them time to reteach material that students had not mastered. One teacher noted, "I don't have time to reteach that because I'll fall behind and we won't be able to cover the next lesson, which they need in order to do well on the next test." Teachers and administrators struggled to figure out how to make time for reteaching in the district's pacing plan; for example, departments debated the merits of actually reteaching at the end of a unit versus "sneaking" the content that needed to be covered again into the next unit.

Some teachers in district A perceived flexibility in spite of the mandate to follow the plan. One noted that the teachers respected each other as professionals, and therefore their judgments to sometimes go more slowly than the pacing chart indicated were also respected because it was in the students' best interests. When discussing benchmark assessment results, some teachers explained that their students didn't do well on particular standards because they had not had time to cover them; as one teacher put it, "everyone's fine with that."

In sum, curricular guidelines provided consistency across each district, and lesson plans served as resources for teachers. Both proved to be important tools. Schools and teachers had some flexibility to make instructional changes based on students' needs, particularly if they could make a case for the deviations with data. This flexibility acknowledged the capacity of teachers to make important instructional decisions on the basis of data and their own professional judgments about what is best for the students in their classrooms. This is an important lesson for data-informed leaders.

Routines: Benchmark Assessments

All three districts in our study connected their districtwide curricula to benchmark assessments, another routine associated with data use. Although the case presented at the beginning of the chapter tells a slightly different story, the three districts we studied tended to report more positive than negative outcomes when it came to the implementation of the benchmark assessments. They had the benefit of allowing teachers to have discussions about student learning and to compare ideas for teaching across their classes. In some cases, however, teachers saw such assessments as information for the district rather than as information they could use for their own formative purposes. Here we share the best-case scenarios as well as some of the pitfalls that districts faced as they attempted to make benchmarks part of their schools' routines.

Development of Benchmark Assessments

District A is an interesting case to examine because its benchmark assessment development process began at the school level rather than the district level. In 2003, an independent consultant worked with one of the high schools to develop benchmark assessments and convinced the principal to focus less on the end result (how the assessments turned out) and more on the process. In the end, this turned out to be a key factor in garnering teacher buy-in to the process of data-informed decision making. The principal reflected, "To be honest, one of the most powerful discussions came from discussing, 'What is mastery?' I think the teachers really bought into it largely because they got to make some of those decisions."

When the district became interested in benchmark assessments more broadly, they envisioned that the tests would serve as a guidepost for future instruction and indicate student progress toward the standards. As they developed and implemented the assessments, they made several key decisions:

- The district drew on the tests that had been developed by teachers at a local high school.

- The district used four benchmark assessments over the year rather than administering them every six weeks. They believed the quarterly assessments would keep the district on track but would also give schools flexibility to have their own school- and teacher-created assessments.

- The district specified a particular five-day window in which to administer the assessment, but allowed individual schools (and even individual teachers) to decide when each test would be given during that week.

- The district was very careful about how and what types of data would be shared across the district. Teacher-level data were initially shared only with principals and individual teachers. Teachers then shared their data in grade-level teams.

- The district pledged to the schools that they would receive their data within two or three days.

- Teachers could access the data electronically, but the district also offered paper reports to make the process more user-friendly for those who were uncomfortable using computers. They did not want the lack of technical knowledge to hinder the practice of using data.

Teachers appreciated this flexibility, but it also introduced some challenges. Because most of the teachers wanted to maximize curriculum coverage before the exams, they tended to administer the tests on the last day of the five-day window they were given. As a result, some students were administered as many as six benchmark tests on a single day. One teacher suggested it might have been better if each department was required to administer their assessment on a particular day. If they were thoughtfully scheduled, the tests could be spread out much more than typically occurred.

Usefulness of Benchmark Assessments

District A hoped that teachers would use the benchmark assessment data to inform their instruction. Unfortunately, district administrators believed that the predominant feeling among teachers was that the benchmarks were administered "so that the district can check on [them]." This belief existed even at the high school, where teachers had created benchmarks before the district. The district worked hard to convince teachers that the benchmarks helped to predict performance on the state test, even beginning with elementary school teachers who were shown the cumulative impact of student performance over time.

District C also faced challenges with its benchmark assessments, especially at the beginning. These assessments, administered every six weeks, were originally designed by the district but were subsequently coproduced by an external provider. District C was trying to align student grades with the benchmarks and state assessments, particularly at the high school level, where students were expected to pass state exit exams. A district administrator noted, "It gets very embarrassing for a principal to have to explain to a parent, 'Your child has made all A's and B's, but he can't pass this test.'"

Frequent student assessments were meant to ensure that students were not falling through the cracks. Although the district had not conducted formal correlation studies, a district administrator believed that the tests were an accurate predictor of performance on the state test.

Benchmark assessments were useful in assessing students' progress toward the standards. Ongoing feedback regarding student mastery enabled teachers to gauge whether a concept or skill was learned rather than simply taught. For example, a science teacher remarked about the utility of the benchmark assessment in pointing out an area of student weakness: "I saw that my kids bombed in the middle. . . . I stopped [and retaught the content]. I would have never stopped had I not looked at their benchmark scores." Thus, the data allowed teachers to guide their reflection about the strengths and weaknesses of their instructional practices. One teacher explained:

> Having a standard, having a goal, does make sure that you are all on the same page and does make sure that you are teaching them something. That's where I think the data are helpful and useful. That's what I like about doing the analysis. I think that there is a part of me that thinks, "Oh wow, why did we get a 56 percent on that one question? Why did no one get that question right?"

But the frequent testing that can accompany an overreliance on assessments can lead to frustration and fatigue for both teachers and students. One teacher lamented, "Kids just feel like 'test, test, test, test, test.'" Teachers also expressed concern regarding how the material measured on the tests shaped what happened in the classroom. As we noted earlier, teachers mentioned that their instruction was influenced by the national policy push to emphasize math and literacy. One performing arts teacher explained: "[With] No Child Left Behind . . . the focus isn't always [on] what's best for the student and what's best for that particular curriculum."

Teachers mentioned that their instruction was influenced by the national policy push to math and literacy.

The presence of benchmark assessments served as an important structural support to help teachers plan and pace their instruction as a group, but they were by no means sufficient when used for formative purposes. To be sure, most teachers followed through with the mandate to administer and analyze benchmark assessments and create action plans on the basis of the data. But they also relied on a wider variety of assessment data—as well as their own intuition—to inform their understanding of student learning. We describe this in more detail in chapter 5.

Regarding benchmark assessments in particular, two key lessons for leaders emerge from our study:

- Benchmark assessments may enable teachers to establish the routine of analyzing assessment data and adjusting instruction accordingly, but they are not enough. Teachers need to consult multiple forms of data on student learning, including types of data that can inform instruction more immediately, such as quick teacher-made assessments at the end of each class. Teachers also need to draw on assessments that allow insight into students' conceptual understandings, as benchmark assessments may be limited in this respect.[9]

- The utility of assessments for informing instruction depends a great deal on implementation. Ideally, teachers should be involved in the creation or at least selection of the assessments, as well as in developing the guidelines about their administration. Otherwise benchmark assessments will be seen as a district surveillance activity rather than as a tool to inform instruction.

Tools: Data Management Systems

Web-based data management systems can be incredibly helpful for distributing data in a timely and efficient manner. Each of the three districts in our study had a system that allowed teachers to access data and forms to guide their reflection and action planning, and these systems served as an important tool for data-informed decision making. They evolved and were used slightly differently in each of the three districts.

District B's data management system gave teachers access to students' standardized test scores, attendance, grades, and other pertinent information. Teachers could also use the system as a grade book, which allowed them to track student performance on classroom-level assessments. Teachers mentioned using the system to access student data to help explain student performance patterns. District C also allowed users to obtain students' scores and reports, including state and local assessments, student profiles, and student transcripts. Its system included the scope and sequence of the curriculum, aligned lessons, and other resources and materials. It enabled users to conduct immediate data disaggregation and item analysis. The hope was that teachers would use it regularly and often, but during the period of our study, quite a few teachers were still struggling to get accustomed to using it. One principal explained that there "there were a lot of growing pains" with the system, and teachers complained that it created more work for them.

District A was one of the early forerunners in using a Web-based data warehouse system that enabled users to access student achievement and demographic data. Teachers were asked to log on to the system to analyze the data for students in their classes before the beginning of the school year and plan their instruction accordingly. For example, one teacher noted that the information helped her identify students who were English learners, which would be useful for constructing seating arrangements of heterogeneously grouped students who could support one another in peer work. During the school year, teachers were expected to generate reports related to student achievement on the district's benchmark assessments. While some teachers we interviewed were comfortable with the system, others were not yet at that stage. One had encountered difficulties in simply logging on and noted that the key challenges for the school's use of data were mechanical: "Getting the program to work, to be accessible, to get it updated, and getting it so that every teacher is on there." Having the technological infrastructure to use programs on a mass scale is an important consideration.

In the years since our study was completed, the user-friendliness of data management systems is likely to have improved considerably. The provider market for such systems has also expanded, leading some districts to abandon less sophisticated systems in favor of others with more capacity. Data-informed leaders would be wise to carefully research options before investing in such tools and certainly involve teachers and other end users in the selection process.

Routines: Structured Time for Collaboration

An important component of effective data use is the opportunity for teachers to share ideas about what the data show and to plan instructional changes together.

Making Collaboration Happen

All three districts thought making time for collaboration was an essential part of encouraging data-informed decision making among teachers. For example, district A established weekly data-centered discussions among faculty, and administrators considered these meetings to be "sacred." The district provided collaboration time every second Wednesday morning, from 7:30 to 9:00. Students arrived at school at 9:30, allowing teachers thirty minutes from the end of the meeting to the beginning of their instructional day. School administrators intentionally built in this transition time because they did not want teachers to feel rushed and thus tempted to use data discussion time for class preparation. Teachers met in grade-level, course-alike groups (e.g., all teachers of ninth-grade English) for the data discussions. The focus of the meetings alternated between data analysis and action planning on the basis of data. District B took a similar approach: every Wednesday morning was dedicated to teacher meetings thanks to a late start school schedule. Teachers met in department or grade-level teams to examine data during some of these established meeting times. Whole faculty meetings also happened on a rotating basis during this time as well, as did occasional professional development sessions.

District C had different structures for data discussion meetings at the elementary and secondary levels. In the elementary school we studied, collaborative lesson planning meetings were conducted every Friday for fifty-five minutes during instructional hours. Schools were required by law to provide forty-five minutes, but the principal managed to provide an additional ten minutes by using a rotation system for physical education and music instruction. The principal considered the planning meetings to be mandatory while the administrative meetings were scheduled with more flexibility.

At the secondary level in district C, all core teachers had daily structured meeting times. The school we studied had a seven-period day that included a mandatory daily planning period when teachers met in departments and another period for individual planning. For example, in the language arts department, two days of the week were focused on data and lessons plans, one day was used to create common assessments, and the other days varied and could be used to bring in speakers, to model lessons, and so forth. When data were discussed, teachers were expected to bring with them specified materials and data and walk through a protocol for data analysis. We describe this process in greater detail later in this chapter.

The Value of Collaboration

The data discussion meetings at all schools across the three districts were meant to allow teachers to jointly examine data with the intent of instructional improvement. More specifically, teachers were tasked with examining data from benchmark or quarterly assessments, considering what might have led to the results, and engaging in joint instructional planning. One teacher explicitly stated that the expected outcome of the data discussion was "modification of instruction." A teacher at another school believed that the connections between the agenda for instructional change and data use were important because "data is only good [if] you understand it and you analyze it, and then it's only good [if] you do something about it."

We often heard from teachers that when it comes to data-informed decision making, "you can't do it alone" and "we do it together." One teacher remarked, "I love our collaboration time," and noted that "we've hit upon the right amount of time" for collaboration. Another said that while looking at "the numbers" did not inspire her, the opportunity to compare results with colleagues and share instructional strategies that arose out of the data discussions was very useful. She said that teachers were comfortable sharing their results and their lessons, and she wished there were more collaboration time for that purpose:

> That's what we're excited about—sharing lessons, sharing great ideas that the kids got, ideas that the kids understood. . . . "Hey, I did a really fun lesson on character; try it!" "Hey, I did an interesting lesson on ambiguity; try it." "Oh cool, you know my kids have already struggled with that. I'd love to try it." Who wouldn't want new strategies, new ideas?

Focusing on data helped teachers orient their discussions around student achievement rather than other agendas. One teacher talked about the importance of using data because "without looking at data, you have everybody just putting their two cents in. Anecdotal evidence is absolutely valuable, but it is really so all over the place. If you start with the data, then everybody's at this one meeting point." In other words, the focus on data encouraged a common understanding among teachers.

> *The focus on data encouraged a common understanding among teachers.*

Teachers were highly aware of their responsibilities within and across grade-level teams. Specifically, they stressed the importance of alignment and accountability as students move up through the grades. A teacher shared, "If I need something from first grade, kindergarten, they're willing to do it." In other words, if a second-grade teacher made suggestions for instruction so that students would be better prepared, the teachers at the prior grade levels were generally willing to oblige. Another teacher remarked that she enjoyed meeting with teachers in other grade levels and figuring out how to align expectations. For some, the formal collaboration time led to informal meetings as well. A teacher in district C, for example, described a conversation during lunchtime when she and her partner compared students' progress.

Leaders took great care to promote the thoughtful use of data, promote a positive and collective orientation toward data use, and provide tools that would help teachers meet the intended goals of collaboration around data use. Even with contextual conditions that shaped their collaborative work in mostly positive ways, teachers at times saw these same conditions as constraints. The lesson here is that structured teacher collaboration time needs to be seen as purposeful. As we consider the future of teacher collaboration as part of school improvement, the data-informed leader must continually check on how collaborative efforts are proceeding, lest they move toward "contrived collegiality."[10] In the end, "collaboration and restructuring can be helpful or harmful, and their meanings and realizations therefore need to be inspected repeatedly to ensure that their educational and social benefits are positive."[11]

Tools: Protocols to Guide Data-Informed Decision Making

While creating the time for educators to collaborate on data use efforts is a vital first step, it is not always sufficient. Districts and schools also employed other tools to guide the data-informed decision making process.

All three districts developed or adopted data discussion protocols in order to ensure that teachers' discussions about classroom-level data occurred and that they could take action based on these conversations. These forms typically guided teachers through a process that began with a discussion of basic trends and then went into more detail regarding strengths, weaknesses, grade-level or course trends, and trends by subgroup. Teachers were asked to prepare ahead of time by filling out data summary sheets. At times they were also required to bring in actual assessments (e.g., pre- and posttests, benchmarks, or unit tests). Within the group meeting, teachers were expected to reflect on the results (and sometimes the tests themselves) and share what appeared to work well, which areas had challenges, and their action plans for improvement.

As one teacher in district A explained, their data discussions addressed questions including: "What did the majority of students do well on? Do you have an explanation for that? What strategies did you use? What level of Bloom's taxonomy [was that]?"[12] The teachers also carefully examined the assessments themselves, asking questions such as, "How was this question worded? Do these kids know what the words in the question mean?" This was important, one teacher believed, in order to understand what might explain varying achievement levels. During the team meetings, teachers sometimes also shared class report graphs or item analysis graphs.

Similarly, schools in district C used a root causes reflection form developed during the district's work with an external professional development trainer.[13] Staff members were asked to generate hypotheses to explain the percentage of students failing as well as to describe what specific interventions were used and whether they were successful. The form also asked staff members what actions they could implement to improve student performance. Specific examples of the types of instructional changes teachers made are presented in chapter 5.

District A used a rubric developed collaboratively by a group of teachers to guide teacher "data walks" around the school. One teacher explained, "We do those walk-arounds where groups of teachers go into other classrooms and watch the teachers teach and see if they can get some ideas." Teachers traveled in teams to observe each other, noting, for example, the classroom environment, how instructional strategies were being used, how the standards were reflected, and the students' engagement level. The data walks were not mandatory. Teachers could sign up if they wanted to be observed and observe others. The school's data team leader described these as opportunities for teachers to observe and then to discuss what they saw.

Many teachers described productive work that emerged from these data discussion protocols. In other cases, however, the administrative regulation that accompanied the protocols led some groups of teachers to focus on the specific tasks (e.g., completing a form to describe the outcomes of their discussions) rather than to have more meaningful discussions around data. For example, in one data team meeting we observed, the overall point of the meeting appeared to be making sure that all parts of the protocol were discussed. With the focus on form completion, teachers spent less time engaging in a discussion of future instructional activities. At the culmination of the meeting, one teacher filled in the last part of the protocol and exclaimed, "Yay, we're done!" revealing the burden these protocols can present for some teachers who see the task as something that takes away from other important activities. In another data team discussion we observed, teachers quickly completed the protocol at the beginning of their meeting using one-word answers and then spent the remainder of their time in a productive discussion of instructional strategies. Thus, in neither case did the protocol itself meet its intended goals. This is an important reminder that these and other tools can promote teachers' opportunities to learn, but if they are formulaic, at best they may take time away from productive conversations and, at worst, limit the spontaneous learning that can occur among teachers.[14] Leaders need to remember that discussions about data may help form the basis for teacher peers sharing their practices, but this is not likely to occur if such conversations are overly constrained. A delicate balance is required, as the protocols need to inspire genuine inquiry around data, rather than compliance.

To Sum Up

A set of goals, routines, and tools is needed to support data use within schools and districts. Well-meaning educational leaders face potentially large successes and failures when implementing seemingly simple tools and procedures designed to aid in the data use process. All of these features have to be carefully planned and delicately put into place so that they achieve their intended goals, lest they end up serving as barriers to data-informed decision making or, worse, negative contributors to student achievement and teacher professionalism.

New goals, routines, and tools are important, but they are not enough to sustain educators' involvement with new data use practices. The tools need to prompt users' thinking and action, and attention to context is critical.[15] As Ikemoto and Honig note, "Whether materials function as a tool depends in part on whether they help users deepen their engagement with particular ideas."[16] Leaders or external consultants can provide assistance to practitioners in modeling how to use the tools for their intended purposes and in making the research ideas in the tools more explicit. Ideally, such assistance includes social opportunities for teachers to grapple with the tools and the ideas embedded within them.

Questions for Discussion

The following questions are intended to guide data-informed leaders in thinking about goals, routines, and tools:

- Are there already meaningful and measurable student achievement goals at the district, school, and classroom levels? Do they provide a focus for data-informed decision making? Do these goals inadvertently narrow the curriculum? If such goals do not exist, how can the lessons in this chapter provide a starting point for engaging stakeholders in the development of meaningful and measurable goals?

- Does the district have a systemwide curriculum that is aligned with the standards (in most US states, the Common Core Standards)? Is it accompanied by flexibility so that teachers can adjust instruction in response to data?

- Are benchmark assessments in place? Has teacher feedback been gathered on the usefulness of the assessments? Do teachers have vehicles by which to educate leaders on what information is most useful in guiding improvements in teaching and learning? If such assessments are not in place, how can the district work to engage teachers in developing or selecting benchmark assessments?

- Is a user-friendly data management system in place? How often is it revisited? Are mechanisms in place to gather teachers' ongoing feedback about the system?

- Is structured time for teacher collaboration provided? Do protocols exist to facilitate teacher discussions around data? Has teacher feedback been gathered to ensure that the protocols facilitate inquiry and are not overly constraining? If collaboration time and protocols do not exist, what lessons in this chapter can be helpful in establishing them?

Chapter 5

Using Data for Instructional Improvement

As she contemplated her move from one high school to another to take on the role of math department chair, Darlene was struck by the differences at the two schools in terms of students' math proficiency scores on the state's standardized test. Both schools had seen math proficiency rise over the past four years, but the scores at Knox, her new school, remained abysmally low. About to assume the position of department chair, Darlene realized that she would need to quickly wrap her head around the discrepancies. The differences appear in table 5.1.

Darlene knew well that the two schools served rather different student populations, though both were very diverse. Eighty-five percent of the students at Knox qualified for free or reduced-price lunches, compared to 45 percent of the students at Grove. Almost 30 percent of the students at Knox were English language learners, compared to 9 percent at Grove. Knox served a student

Table 5.1. Math Proficiency Rates at Knox and Grove High Schools, 2008–2011

Year	Percent Proficient in Math at Knox High School	Percent Proficient in Math at Grove High School
2011	6%	45%
2010	5	37
2009	4	35
2008	2	29

population that was primarily Latino and African American, whereas Grove's student population was over 50 percent Asian and almost 20 percent white.

Some educators faced with making sense of these data on student proficiency and demographics would look no further. They would conclude that since Knox served a student population that was poor and predominantly black and Latino, they would have predictably lower scores than Grove. After all, this fits with national achievement trends. In essence, they would blame the students' backgrounds for their underachievement and make excuses about the impossibility of dramatically raising proficiency rates. Unfortunately, this happens in some schools, where rather than taking responsibility for improving student achievement, educators point fingers at the students themselves or their families. This deficit perspective is a central problem in urban education and a land mine on the route to effective data use.

Fortunately, Darlene did not fall into this trap. She dug much deeper into the data to look for explanations for the achievement trends and to develop her action plan. She looked at course-taking patterns at the two schools and found dramatically different numbers of students taking algebra 1 and intermediate algebra. Looking closely at the test scores over multiple years, she concluded that Knox students were promoted into intermediate algebra without having shown even a basic algebra or geometry proficiency. In fact, 70 to 80 percent were in the below-basic or basic category. Digging still deeper, she learned that Knox had a policy of placing students into geometry in ninth grade regardless of whether they had passed algebra in eighth grade. In essence, students were being moved through courses without the skills to be successful at the next level, and this greatly inhibited their chances of success.

Informed by these data, Darlene developed an action plan for the Knox math department. She focused first on a system of more accurate student placement. All students would be assessed in the spring of eighth grade or the beginning of ninth grade using a well-validated math diagnostic assessment, and they would be placed accordingly. Darlene also developed clearly defined course pathways to college that required a redesign of the master schedule. She wanted to ensure that regardless of entry point, all students would graduate having completed the courses required for college access in the state. She also assembled a data team to collaboratively develop measures of success to track the math department's progress toward these goals. Fortunately, she had the support of a principal, new to the school, who was also motivated toward achieving dramatic educational improvement at Knox.[1]

Thoughtful data-informed decision making—and, more specifically, data-informed leadership—involves more than collecting and looking at student achievement data. A deep process of inquiry using multiple sources and types of data is essential in developing instructional plans that will improve student achievement. Different student performance data lend themselves to informing different types of concerns and decision making processes.

Educators must look beyond their taken-for-granted assumptions to critically present and assess alternative explanations and gather more data before leaping to solutions or answers. Most important, they must think deeply about their practices, especially around issues of access, class placement, and pedagogy. The thoughtful use of data for instructional decision making cannot be divorced from reflection about one's beliefs, assumptions, and practices around how students learn.

> *The thoughtful use of data cannot be divorced from reflection about one's beliefs, assumptions, and practices around how students learn.*

External, schoolwide, and classroom assessments all function differently.[2] While external assessments may provide initial direction to help identify struggling students, develop improvement plans, or set long-term goals, schoolwide assessments help refine instructional strategies and adjust professional development needs throughout the year. Classroom assessments, especially formative assessments, provide immediate, flexible, and custom data to guide day-to-day practices. Margaret Heritage notes that formative assessments have four elements: identifying the learning gap, providing feedback, enabling student involvement, and linking to learning progression.[3] Activities range from teachers' observations of students during tasks to classroom discussions, classroom tests, and student self-reflections. Research on formative assessments demonstrates that activities such as checking for student understanding, providing student feedback, increasing wait time for student response, enabling student self-reflection, and asking higher-order questions all contribute to learning.[4] Day-to-day instructional and student engagement data are particularly useful for teachers.

Developing the skills and capacity to engage in thoughtful inquiry processes with data is not always straightforward or easily accomplished, however. In addition to the structural and cultural supports at the district and school levels that we mentioned in previous chapters, teachers may require specific sets of knowledge, experiences, and examples to use data productively.[5] Teachers need to develop the ability to engage in systematic inquiry—skills that are not necessarily built into their professional development.[6] In addition, not all educators currently have the data literacy skills to formulate questions about data, assess different types of data, interpret results, and develop action plans.[7]

In this chapter, we share some of the ways in which teachers in our study engaged in data-informed instructional decision making. All were working in schools and systems where there was overwhelming consensus about the importance of using data to improve teacher performance and student achievement. They used data at the classroom level because they believed that these data allowed them to better meet their students' learning needs. We highlight the varied types of data they used to inform their action planning around instructional improvement and share some examples of how reflecting on data influenced their practices.

Using Multiple Types of Data Tied to Learning and Teaching Goals

The data-informed decision-making process must include clear learning goals accompanied by valid assessments and different types of data. As we mentioned in chapter 4, the data that teachers and administrators relied on informed how they measured learning. For many, learning was defined as progress toward the state standards. For example, a high school math teacher in district A said that the interim assessment was useful "because it allows me to see what standards I need to focus on and whether they're improving or not." An English teacher at the school reiterated, "I'm really trying hard to go back to the standards that the majority of the class hasn't hit on. . . . Let's see if I can teach it in a different way. Or maybe that's where I can talk to other teachers and ask how they did that." One teacher consulted with her students after identifying weakness areas, asking them what she could do to teach the material more effectively.

Teachers and administrators grappled with measuring students' progress toward goals that were not measured by the standards. District A leaders, for example, were concerned that although proficiency rates on the state test had gone up dramatically in the past five years, the college preparatory course completion rates had not changed. To address this discrepancy, district leaders asked teachers and counselors to rely much more on data when placing students into courses. Rather than relying solely on grades and intuition as they had done in the past, teachers were asked to support placement recommendations with state scores and benchmark assessment data. The result was that more students were placed into more challenging classes.

At the same high school, multiple types of student achievement data were used regularly and in different ways: state test scores, benchmark and midquarter interim assessment results, language proficiency test scores, high school exit exam passing rates, Advanced Placement passing rates, and placement in college preparatory course work. They also used student grades, particularly noting the number of Ds and Fs that students received. The school also used data from the walk-arounds that we described in chapter 4.

Data do not need to be limited to formal assessments. At the classroom level, for example, teachers relied on formal and informal data to keep track of student progress. An English teacher in district A said that she turned to vocabulary quizzes, chapter tests, graphic organizers, essays, and even her own notes to create a full picture of student achievement in order to guide her instruction: "Everything we do in here gets looked at by me. How do you give a kid something and then tell him, 'I'm not going to look at it; it's not important?' Some of them are just notes, but we go over it and verbally we assess: 'Are we on the same page? Are we understanding?'" A science teacher said she relied on students' grades on her own tests, lab reports, informal assessments, and "talking to the kids. That's most important. I have to know my kids." She made a point of knowing all 175 of her students. To a lesser degree, she also consulted the results from interim and benchmark assessments because they were useful in assessing the knowledge of students who "don't perform" on class assignments.

At a high school in district B, teachers used benchmarks as a formative assessment tool, but they also used their own teacher-selected or teacher-created assessments and simple checks of student understanding as guideposts for instruction. They checked homework and pop quizzes to gauge students' understanding of class material. During our classroom observations, we also saw teachers walking around and checking student work, collecting samples during lessons, directing students to write responses on whiteboards during lessons in order to check for understanding, and listening to students as they helped each other. In daily informal assessments about student learning, teachers observed student responses to know what was effective and what was not. In addition, two department chairs mentioned asking students to give them verbal feedback on some lessons in order to help them plan for future classes. Some teachers engaged students by asking for feedback on their instructional practices.

How Data Use Changes Classroom Practices: Pausing, Reflecting, and Reteaching

Many of the teachers and administrators in our study looked at a broad array of data to inform classroom practices, although the degree to which standardized assessments (e.g., state tests and district benchmarks) were emphasized varied by state and district. Here we share multiple examples of how thoughtful data use moved beyond consideration of student achievement data to include course placement trends, formative assessments, and observations of both student and teacher behaviors. These examples reinforce that the process of examining data can propel positive changes in classroom practices—a process that requires reflecting on both data and existing instructional practices.

Teachers drew on their own expertise to move beyond a single data point (e.g., test results) to look at student behavior and their own teaching practices. In district C, a fourth-grade teacher noticed that as her students practiced for a standardized state test, one student's reading scores fluctuated from 30 percent to 75 percent. Viewing this as a red flag and a puzzle, the teacher observed the student's test-taking abilities and his responses to the testing environment. She watched his behavior and examined her own, and she realized that some of the test-taking strategies that she had been practicing with her students were slowing him down even further. She concluded, "I cannot push him." Ultimately she realized she needed to focus on verbal encouragements to help improve his focus. This example speaks to the importance of the teacher's reflections and observations as data that should be part of the inquiry process in conjunction with student performance data. Teaching and learning are interactive; they do not take place in a vacuum.

Similar examples at other schools highlight the importance of examining student performance data and trends in context. Staff at a different school in district C used various types of data to pinpoint whether the roots of specific problems were at the school, department, teacher, or student subgroup level, including observations of teacher-student interactions, to understand concerns or problems not just with academic performance but also with student engagement. For example, the assistant principal noticed that Latino students were not performing well across one teacher's classes. Digging deeper into the data patterns, it became clear that specifically Latino male students were not doing well. She had a discussion with the teacher who was of Latino heritage himself. He admitted that he was harder on them, not because he didn't care but because he had high expectations of them. As a next step, she filmed his classes and reviewed the footage with him. He was surprised to see that he was raising his voice at students frequently. Afterward he worked with intervention specialists to learn new strategies for classroom management.

Without pausing, reflecting, and collecting more data, it would have been easy to mistakenly conclude that this teacher was not concerned about this group of students, and that was causing their lower grades. It would also have been easy for the assistant principal to simply believe, based on the patterns in one data source, that the teacher was ineffective. But this would not have helped her understand why he had trouble or how she could support his professional development. Talking with him and listening to his perceptions and beliefs about working with students started a dialogue about why this group of students was consistently underperforming in all of his classes. Helping him observe and reflect on his own practices pinpointed specific behaviors that he needed to change. This extended process of inquiry started with student performance data but did not end there. It was a joint reflection and problem-solving process between the teacher and administrator rather than a simple evaluative one.

The inquiry process is at the core of using data thoughtfully, and assessing student engagement is at the heart of what counts as critical data for instructional improvement. We saw that the most salient information that affected instruction at the high school in district B came from the data gathered informally on a daily basis by teachers. They mentioned walking around and checking student work, reflecting on student responses to lessons to see if the students could be doing something more effectively, and asking students about teaching techniques that they found to be either effective or ineffective. Teachers also observed the level of student engagement in the learning activities. One teacher explained how the informal data contributed to ongoing reflection:

> I think teaching is not, "At the end of the day, you're done."
> You're constantly thinking about it. You go home and you
> wonder, "Why didn't that go well, or why did that go well?"
> You make a mental note, or you write it on your lesson: "We
> need to change that for next [time]." Or the next day you make
> the change: "You know what, you guys, what I taught you yes-
> terday, we should probably have done it this way."

In fact, many teachers explained that having greater knowledge of their students' performance levels led them to think about experimenting with new instructional strategies. Through such strategies, they attempted to address the learning needs of different students in the classroom. An English teacher in district A noted that she employed a variety of instructional techniques to reach the diverse learning styles of students across her classes: "I do a lot of differentiating—group work, individual, graphic organizers, and overhead board—because my students' learning styles vary so much." She gave an example:

> Yesterday I did an interesting hands-on assignment introducing character, which is our next chapter. The kids loved it. I'm so excited to see where this is going to take us. I brought magazine pictures, and we were basically stereotyping or judging people based on the pictures [and on] their looks from the pictures—not necessarily just the physical, but digging deeper.

When asked what data drove the decisions to use particular techniques, she mentioned the state test results, though she acknowledged their limitations. She also observed how long it takes students to complete assignments and how they respond to particular kinds of activities. She relied on her own learning experiences to inform her decisions about how to instruct students: "I can see the kids who are really into the graphic organizers; they need something right there physically while we're doing something. For instance, today we're going to be using our interactive reader, which is their workbook that has stories in it that they can physically underline, write in the margins." She believed that note taking in the workbooks would also help improve students' active engagement in the learning process and retention of the new material.

Moving toward Student Engagement as the Center of Instructional Improvement

Our observations in the districts and schools convinced us that improving student engagement, in concert with developing teachers' knowledge and skills, must be at the center of efforts to improve instruction. Educators at two sites found that gathering and analyzing data specific to student engagement provided a powerful tool to improve students' involvement in their own learning. Sharing assessment data with students in the classroom also appeared to increase students' ownership of their goals and plans for improvement, and many teachers experimented with different ways of doing this. Efforts to improve teaching and learning through the use of data invited students to play an active role in contributing to their own academic growth and learning environment. This is not to say that we observed high levels of student engagement across all sites, but rather that we were impressed by the efforts of some educators to make improving student engagement a pillar of their reform efforts.

Educators who believed that improved student achievement evolves from shared understandings and goals about student learning also recognized that students themselves had to be involved in the process. During our observations in district B, for example, students were not yet involved in the data-informed decision-making process in systematic ways, though several teachers mentioned the importance of having students look at their own data. This was a change from the past when, as one teacher said, "there was no accountability for the child."

Teachers also involved the students in data collection and analysis. For example, the social studies department chair had his students track their own progress on exams and collect their own data in order to identify their own weaknesses—a skill he believed was important to develop because he saw it as relevant to life beyond high school. In math, students received test scores that reflected whether they had demonstrated mastery on particular outcomes. Two teachers mentioned sharing the results of the class so that students could learn how their performance compared to that of others.

Central office administrators can also take the lead in improving student engagement and voice across the school system. Although district A, for example, focused on hard data, these educators also saw the value in other types of data, including classroom observations, to understand students and their needs. Several district administrators and school personnel had begun informally mentoring students to provide a helping hand to those who might be struggling. In the course of the mentoring, district personnel attended classes with the students they were mentoring to see things through the eyes of their students. Shadowing students helped leaders who were no longer in the classroom stay connected with the challenges that students faced and the challenges teachers had when trying to engage students in classroom instruction. The program led the district to develop ways to help students develop self-regulation strategies that would improve their opportunities for success in high school and beyond. The superintendent explained, "Our big issue is, how do we get our students to become active participants in their own learning?" Instead of simply asking students to get more engaged, the focus in the district was to "set up some classroom procedures and a sense of inquiry so that students feel vested, that they are engaged, that we start to pull them in, and then get them to be more self-sufficient."

The district A high school we studied made a big instructional push to get students to take ownership of their own learning, and this was being achieved in part through the use of data in the classroom. One English teacher described "putting up pie charts" of assessment results for the whole class to see and said that she and her colleagues were asking students to look at their the results themselves, note their strengths and weaknesses, and write reflections on "what strategies they can use themselves to meet the standard. . . . That's a great way to use these data." She believed that this "opens up that dialogue" with the teacher, because it allows a student to then say, "I need this from you too." In one of her classes, students were writing action plans for their portfolios, and the teacher was hoping to revisit the plans with students at the end of each quarter to discuss whether they followed through and what results they achieved. She thought this was particularly important for failing students who needed to take some initiative to chart their improvement. English teachers at the school also used a self-assessment form in writing that asked students to reflect on their strengths and weaknesses and list steps they may be able to take to improve their writing, as well as note where they needed clarification on scores or comments their teacher had made.

Efforts to engage students in data analysis and reflection were also undertaken at the elementary school level. One school in district A drafted a self-assessment form entitled, "Think Like a Statistician," in order to help students become familiar with their own assessment data and chart plans for improvement. The form asked the student to list areas of strength and improvement. It also asked them to mark the practices they had engaged in to support the improvement, including activities that involved working alone, with the teacher, or with a parent or tutor (e.g., "monitored my own progress," "partnered with a classmate," "asked questions for clarification," and "family member/tutor worked with me").

We learned from our cases that efforts to improve student engagement can be enhanced through the use of data in two primary ways. First, data about student engagement and satisfaction can be a source for instructional improvement. These data can be gathered formally through surveys of students or informally through observations of student engagement in the classroom. And second, teachers can use data from assessments and other sources to help students take on a greater degree of ownership of their learning. By examining data, students can become

> *By examining data, students can become more familiar with how they learn and what they have learned.*

more familiar with how they learn and what they have learned. At the high school level, students could also be involved in data use reforms in deeper ways—for example, by being part of conversations about schoolwide data trends.

Data Don't Tell Us Everything

While almost all teachers found assessment data useful for improving instruction, they acknowledged these data did not tell them everything they needed to know in order to help students be successful. Teachers frequently cited affective elements that could not be captured in any type of assessment. One teacher said, "The data tell me a pattern but not what makes students tick." She added, "I want to know students personally. I want to know what makes them tick." Another teacher expressed a similar concern about the overreliance on test data as a way to measure students' learning:

> I have a hard time. I go back and forth looking at these data because I don't necessarily know if they are a true reflection. I may look at the data but don't take them as a whole. I look at the [state test results], okay maybe, but where was that kid coming from? What's that kid's home life like? Do they even have a place to study? Some of them don't. Some of them sleep on the couch or the floor because they've got ten people living in a two-bedroom apartment. So as much as the data tell me, they don't tell me everything. I don't necessarily think it's a true reflection of who they are.

Another teacher in district B also expressed worries about relying too heavily on data in instructional design:

> I don't think you can base your teaching all on data. There will be some kids who maybe don't learn as much as others but they

did gain some material. A lot of kids don't like math when they walk in. If you can change their attitude about it, I think that's more important than data. That's a problem I think with [the state's standardized assessment]. . . . I mean, yes, it's great the kid has passed his state test, but can he use it?

Although almost all of the teachers we spoke with were interested in using data and found them helpful, they were also aware of the limitations: "It's not everything. . . . But it's just another way for us to try and improve and help our kids."

The term *data* has been largely defined in terms of student performance results on district and state assessments, and some teachers believed that there was too much focus on this type of information. To one science teacher in district A, *data* was synonymous with testing, and he believed that the type of learning that he valued could not be measured:

I think we feel, as science teachers, there's an overemphasis on the data. I feel like we are testing our kids beyond reason. It leaves very little for a child to just explore. How do you grade children when you send them out to the horticulture field and ask them to go find an ecosystem, or when you ask them to describe an ecosystem? I'm sorry it's not on the test. It's not in the bubbles. But it's learning.

When student learning was narrowly defined in terms of performance on multiple-choice tests, teachers often felt the tests were geared toward simple recall rather than critical thinking. They also contested the results as "not telling the whole story" and felt it was important to take into consideration emotional and contextual factors—such as students' levels of test anxiety or difficulties at home—when making judgments about student performance. As a result, they viewed observations of student engagement as well as student attitudes and emotional well-being as vital sources of information."

School leaders and teachers must understand their major purposes and roles as educators. One assistant principal in district B put it clearly and succinctly: "We're dealing with our children; we're not dealing with making money. We're not dealing with profit. That's the fundamental difference between our business and every other business in the world. Our bottom line is trying to create a society that works." Teachers also stressed the importance of building relationships with students to ensure their progress. One social studies teacher said, "I think one of the greatest strengths that a teacher can have is the relationships you build with your students. I think there's nothing greater that I do than that." Several teachers echoed this concern that individual students should not get lost in the numbers and that teaching is about building relationships, not just correctly implementing techniques or transmitting content.

> *One assistant principal put it clearly and succinctly: "Our bottom line is trying to create a society that works."*

Building Instructional and Data Use Knowledge and Skills: Challenges and Supports

The teachers we observed and spoke with saw the value in data use as they experienced successes and improvement efforts, even as they also remained aware of the limitations of data for informing their classroom instruction. But they faced some challenges as they struggled with making decisions on the basis of data. The experiences of these teachers remind us that data do not ultimately determine how teachers deal with individual student needs. Data may give teachers a picture of student progress, but they do not tell teachers how to differentiate their instruction accordingly. As one teacher asked, "How am I supposed to teach differently?"

Teacher Development

Although assessments and observations could pinpoint areas for improvement and areas of strength, data alone could not help improve student learning. Without professional development to build instructional knowledge for reteaching, differentiating instruction, and scaffolding students, teachers did not have the tools to use data to make improvements. Thus, building educators' ability to engage in effective data use seemed to go hand-in-hand with building instructional knowledge and skills.

Expressing a sentiment shared by several teachers across school systems, one teacher remarked that gathering and disaggregating data was not the problem, but training on what to do with the data and how to read the data more carefully would be welcomed. Another teacher urged: "Don't just throw the data out there and expect the teachers to be able to pick it up and run with it." Teachers were not the only ones to express a desire for more training, support, and experience on data use. Principals indicated that they too needed to develop the skills and capacity to have "quality conversations" around data. One principal thought it would be helpful to have someone who could be a coach or a critical friend.

Most of the educators in our study highlighted their desire to learn from other educators across school systems. Teachers wanted more opportunities to observe other schools and learn from other teachers so that they could build broader repertoires of instructional strategies. Some specifically mentioned that they would like to see more examples of how other schools were conducting their own data conversations.

Other teachers felt that data did not necessarily lead them to use diverse instructional strategies; in fact, they felt the opposite was true. One teacher said that he felt driven to do whatever was necessary to get more students to pass the state test, and he thought traditional techniques were most effective: "I don't do discovery learning. I don't do cooperative learning. I mean, it's just straight traditional lecture, do, do, analyze, evaluate, grade, hand back, immediate feedback and then we do, do, do." An English teacher who was resistant to using data said that she does not look at those data when planning for instruction: "For me, teaching is to go by your gut instinct. I'm not dealing with numbers. I'm dealing with students. I'm not teaching them for a test; I'm teaching them for college. I'm teaching them for life." She believed that "nothing that the school provides" is helpful for teaching: "It's just using my own background as an English major, I think."

Using data for instructional practice requires more than analyzing data and understanding how to engage in the inquiry process. In addition, training on how to evaluate data does not increase pedagogical skills and content knowledge. Using formative assessment, for example, is an ongoing process that aims to continually assess student learning to close the gap between existing student knowledge and instructional goals. Thus, using data effectively to enhance student learning requires not only assessment knowledge but also domain-specific and pedagogical expertise.[8] It bears repeating that knowing how to analyze data goes hand-in-hand with building instructional capacity. Both require a sophisticated set of skills and knowledge, which educators need to apply in context. This suggests that educators need multiple and sustained opportunities to develop and apply these skills and knowledge.

> *Training on how to evaluate data does not increase pedagogical skills and content knowledge.*

Systemic Support

The schools and districts that participated in our study provided tools and routines that reshaped cultural norms. They also supported teacher data use by devoting significant time, energy, and resources to improving instructional capacity so that teachers could analyze the data and use the resulting information to improve their instructional practices. School leaders and department chairs played a key role in observing instruction on a continuous basis and in helping teachers become more reflective and willing to use data to inform their teaching. The school systems also employed coaches, especially to assist new teachers, and they invested in broad-scale professional development aimed at improving instruction. All of this was a work in progress.

The professional development offered by district A, called Strategy Academy, focused on instructional strategies and data-informed decision making. Teacher representatives from across departments in all of the high schools came together with assistant principals, principals, and counselors three to four times each year for a full day. They discussed, among other things, strategies for writing across content areas, the needs of students reading below grade level and of English learners, academic vocabulary, and student placement. During the period of our study, the group was looking at Achievement Via Individual Determination (AVID) strategies, with a focus on scaffolding students for more self-regulation. AVID strategies included collaborative learning and using writing and inquiry as tools for learning.[9] Although the district leaders had ambitious ideas about what could be done with data (and in educational reform more generally), they were mindful that change must happen incrementally in order to ensure teacher buy-in. As the superintendent shared, "Learning new strategies and better ways to serve students takes time and it takes practice. Even the most committed teachers need time to internalize the strategies if you truly are interested in building capacity."

A district A administrator had also initiated professional development on other instructional strategies. For example, she was working with teachers on questioning techniques (e.g., asking different levels of questions, using spiraling question techniques, and waiting for students to answer). One science teacher reported attending a workshop on how to effectively apply direct instruction and how to coach other teachers to do so as well. Growing out of these district workshops, the teachers at a high school in district A took it on themselves to develop and videotape model lessons on various student engagement strategies, such as how to use a whiteboard for engaging students. The DVDs profiling teacher instructional strategies were distributed schoolwide, and each teacher committed to trying out at least one new strategy in the classroom.

As all of the examples reveal, most of the professional development and capacity-building activities initiated by the systems and schools in our study concentrated on instructional issues rather than other topics. This provides an important lesson for the data-informed leader, because the area where data-informed decision making often falls short is in the phase of acting on the data. Unless teachers are provided with opportunities to expand their toolbox of instructional strategies through professional development and opportunities to learn from and observe each other, it is much less likely that students will receive improved instruction. The risk then is that teachers will use data to find gaps in student learning but then continue to teach in a way that did not work well the first time.

To Sum Up

Using data for instructional improvement is a complex process requiring the development of knowledge of data use and instructional improvement. Consequently, we need to focus attention on multiple types of data and building instructional capacity. The schools and districts in our study acknowledged that this is a continuous improvement process that includes some developmental adjustments and growing pains. At the classroom level, we observed new instructional practices taking hold as a result of these efforts. Teachers used a combination of formal and informal assessments to guide instruction, and careful analysis of data required them to think about new ways to diversify instruction in the classroom. They used a variety of instructional techniques, including group work, frequent individual student check-ins, and practice activities at the beginning of class. Teachers also used innovative techniques to assess student mastery and target instruction accordingly. At the cornerstone of these efforts was the acknowledgment that student engagement is key and that while data are important and powerful tools, they do not always capture the student-teacher relationship that is at the center of learning.

Questions for Discussion

The following discussion questions can guide data-informed leaders in thinking about their efforts in using data for continuous improvement and assisting teachers to use data:

- How can student engagement be stimulated through the use of data?

- What processes could be put into place to ensure that data are being used in thoughtful ways at all levels of the system?

- Are there opportunities for teachers to develop the capacity for using both data and new instructional strategies?

- How are data used for student placement into classes? How could more types of data be brought to bear in order to ensure expanded learning opportunities for students?

- Are there vehicles for teachers to share information with each other about the types of data they use to inform their instruction?

- Are there teachers who are models of using data to inform instruction? How might their practices be shared?

- How might observational data be used to get a better picture of student learning and engagement?

Chapter 6

Facing the Future with Data-Informed Leadership

As we look to the future, we call on leaders to embrace data-informed leadership, an essential form of leadership in this era of accountability and an engine for educational change. The charge of the data-informed leader is critical: she or he must manage a process that involves careful and critical decision making that can have an enormous impact on the learning of students and teachers every day. As we have shown, data use can bring many possibilities for transforming schools and districts, but the data can also be misguided and highly problematic. Fortunately, data-informed leaders do not take on this important role alone. Data-informed leadership is an activity involving many people, not just those in formal leadership positions. Given this complexity, it is important for data-informed leaders to keep the following calls to action, built on the lessons in this book, front and center.

Call #1: Use Data to Support a Culture of Inquiry and Continuous Improvement

The data-informed leader can avoid many of the perils of data use by embedding the data within a culture of continuous improvement. This is not going to be easy given the current accountability context. Data use for school improvement, especially in the United States, have been tightly connected to government accountability policies, and there is little chance of this changing. This is both a promise and a pitfall. The press to improve student achievement on external measures can provide political lever-age and an impetus for leaders to bring teachers and principals on board with data use. However, the integration of accountability with data use has also led to perverse incentives and the problems we explained, including overt cheating, a narrowing of the cur-riculum, and a focus on some children to the exclusion of others. As external accountability demands loom large in the minds of principals and teachers, data-informed leadership requires model-ing and sustained attention to make data use part of a culture of inquiry and continuous improvement. The data-informed leader also plays a key role in supporting the beliefs and norms that enable this focus to take hold.

Rather than promoting a culture of compliance, the data-informed leader needs to enable teachers to take lead roles in mapping curricula, developing assessments, and guiding dis-cussions with their colleagues, all in the service of continuous improvement. Educational change is a social process, and suc-cess is reliant on interdependence among educators and mutual accountability between teachers and school leaders and between school and district leaders. As with any other reform effort that seeks to improve teaching and learning, there is a great need for distributed leadership in data-informed decision making.

Key to building this culture of using data in the service of con-tinuous improvement is encouraging rigorous reflection on a wide array of data on an ongoing basis at all levels of the system. We know that data-informed decision making is not a straightfor-ward, lockstep process. Schools need to rely on data that range from simple to complex, and the questions leaders and teach-ers ask of such data should be wide ranging as well. The data-informed leader needs to lead teachers and others toward being inquiry and analysis focused in their use of data.[1] A key compo-nent of data-informed leadership is moving toward more com-plex definitions of what counts as student learning and of what informs how we think about student learning. Documenting the level of student engagement in the classroom through observations can be more enlightening and lead to innovations in teaching and learning than examining test scores on a page.

Call #2: Use Knowledge of the Four Ps in Planning Reform Efforts

Data-informed leaders must be highly attuned to the four Ps existing in their work contexts: people, policies, practices, and patterns. They must use their knowledge of these aspects of context in their planning of educational change efforts. Plenty of educational reforms have been implemented with insufficient attention to these factors. Reforms then fail to achieve their intended goals. We tend to blame the failures on those who initiated them, not realizing that the success or failure of any reform is often a product of many interactions among many people. It is vital that leaders have a deep understanding of context because it provides both opportunities and constraints.

One strategy for taking on this call is to look for opportunities for understanding the context from different points of view. The system looks very different from the top than it does from the middle or the bottom. Consider the experience of a first-year teacher versus a district leader with years of experience in education and administration. Or imagine what a different perspective a board member would have of the system than would a parent from a community that feels disenfranchised. By understanding how different people—teachers, parents, students—view and experience educational reforms, the data-informed leader can plan and implement reforms much more wisely.

Existing patterns and practices in a school or district can be either transformational or transfixing.[2] The data-informed leader can use data to highlight promising or effective practices so that others can learn from them. The more challenging corollary is to also use data to call attention to problematic practices or patterns of interaction that have previously been unaddressed. The increased level of transparency that this requires involves building trust, part of the next call to action.

Call #3: Build Trust in the Process of Data Use

Trust is a critical element of data-informed leadership. The data-informed leader needs to create a nonthreatening atmosphere around data use. Data must not be used punitively against teachers, principals, or students. Instead, the data-informed leader ought to frame the responsibility for student results in a collective rather than individualistic way. Creating a "we feeling" with respect to student achievement results fits the promotion of collaboration and collegiality as important components of data-informed decision making. At both the school and district levels, data should be reviewed in team settings, with the assumption that a diversity of perspectives will lead to a better analysis of the patterns in the data and a more informed course of action from the analysis. For some teachers, examining data will always be a personal process that may cause them to reflect more deeply on the results for students in their own classrooms. Over time, the goal is for teachers to view multiple forms of data as relevant and necessary to improving classroom instruction and student achievement, rather than as something to fear.

Creating relations of trust between teachers in schools, between teachers and principals, and between schools and the district office is not easy, especially if there is a history of distrust. Trust can be built by fostering a sense of mutual accountability. Leaders need to remind themselves and their staff that the purpose of using data is to raise questions and inform discussions rather than to dictate a course of action.[3] Rather than holding schools accountable in a traditional model of relations between system and school, district leaders can promote the idea that their function is to support the work of the schools. As part of this model, schools should expect that if they are asked to do something new, it is because the data have revealed an area of concern that the innovation might address. So too district leaders could ask that if schools are to make changes, these changes would be supported by data as well. Schools and teachers alike can thus be allowed sufficient autonomy to make decisions, provided they are rooted in evidence that they are aimed toward improving student learning.

Call #4: Build Skills and Knowledge for Data Use

The data-informed leader plays a crucial role in developing and investing in professional capital—people's knowledge, skills at working together, and ability to make wise judgments with respect to data use.[4] As teachers make sense of data use, they are guided by their existing beliefs, their interpretations of new policies and practices, and the contexts of their work. Teachers are also influenced by their interactions with their colleagues and by power relations existing within their schools and districts.[5] These dynamics are important to what happens in the classroom and in meetings when teachers work with each other and with leaders.

For these reasons, mandating change is seldom effective. Leaders need to bring teachers along in a way that acknowledges the demands of data use in the context of their work. The data-informed leader models thoughtful and careful use of data rather than simply asking teachers to jump on a train with an uncertain direction. Strong connections between schools and district office leaders can be useful in framing data use as a synergistic effort that has support across the system. Almost every leader faces the challenge of bringing along staff who have diverse needs and interests. Again here, distributed leadership can aid tremendously in strategically building a culture for change.

The data-informed leader must be prepared to support teachers who need to develop an expanded set of tools for teaching. Teacher professional development in the use of data and in differentiating instruction to meet the needs of all learners is essential, as is time for teachers to work together and share practices. Without support, teachers may be left to chase the numbers, focusing on the improvement of students' achievement on narrow measures rather than providing them with multiple opportunities to learn and be successful. Here again, a high-stakes accountability system that is designed to improve student achievement can inadvertently push some teachers in the wrong direction.

The data-informed leader must also help teachers build decisional capital—"the ability to make wise judgments in circumstances where there is no fixed rule or piece of incontrovertible evidence to guide them."[6] Some teachers struggle with how to incorporate their own knowledge of students and teaching into their decision making. The push to use data to drive decision making has made some teachers feel as though they should not rely on their intuition or what they knew about students based on the relationships they had built with them. These are vitally important sources of knowledge that teachers must be encouraged to continue to use to inform their classroom instruction.

Call #5: Establish Goals, Routines, and Tools to Support Data Use

Data-informed leadership requires the development of new goals, routines, and tools. These structural supports are also essential for the process of data-informed decision making to be successful. Otherwise old routines and ways of doing things may come into conflict with efforts to use data to inform decisions. It is paramount for leaders to pay close attention to the activities in which data use occurs, as these activities provide opportunities for reframing data use and the roles that people play. It is at this point that reculturing and restructuring become intertwined.

The process of establishing goals that are linked to data is as fundamental as the goals themselves. Goal setting at the system, school, and classroom levels serves as an important scaffold of support for data-informed decision making and as a tool to measure progress. As educators become focused on thinking about what they want their students to know and be able to do, they can think more deeply about student learning and how to measure it. With goals in place, they can develop action plans that are continuously revisited and refined. And when the original goals have been met, new goals are developed.

Systemwide curricular guidelines are another significant tool in the data use process that the data-informed leader will need to manage carefully. Teachers can be expected to follow the curriculum, but they also require flexibility (sometimes a great deal of flexibility) to adjust their pacing and teaching methodologies to suit students' needs or respond to issues that arise in their analysis of achievement data. District and school leaders can provide supports in the form of lesson plans that teachers can adapt if they choose to. However, these should be guides rather than mandates. In sum, common guidelines allow all teachers to come to a shared understanding of goals and actions in their discussions about data and, with flexibility, they will also have the autonomy to make decisions on the basis of the data and their professional expertise.

Benchmark assessments can be helpful scaffolds for data use, especially when teachers participate in developing them. These assessments can help get teachers into the routine of analyzing data, although they are by no means sufficient for producing data-informed instruction. Teachers must also be encouraged to use multiple forms of data on student achievement in order to get a full picture of student learning. Advances in technology have made analyzing data easier for teachers. The use of benchmark assessments and technology must be embedded within a culture of continuous improvement because alone they are not sufficient to accomplish the goals of data-informed decision making.

Data-informed leadership also involves providing structured time for collaboration for teachers. Indeed, most teachers view collaboration as a fundamental activity in supporting data use, and it can support the development of professional capital. Teachers can meet in grade level, course-alike, and department teams to examine data and create action plans together. System and school leaders may wish to provide protocols to guide teacher discussions. Most teachers we spoke to believed that they guided productive work around the data, but sometimes the need to complete a form seemed a bit contrived. Again, it is important for the data-informed leader to ask for the assistance of teachers in developing these tools so that they can most effectively engage the people who use them. After all, data use can be both facilitated and constrained by the use of protocols.

The data-informed leader needs to plan and implement these new goals, routines, and tools very thoughtfully in order to help facilitate the data use process and be open to abandoning something if it isn't working well. Careful attention to the four Ps is required. This involves not just anticipating how individuals might take up new tools and routines, but also how groups, each with its own set of dynamics, might use them. A tool or routine that is a relief in one school or district could become an imposition in another.

Call #6: Keep Equity Concerns at the Forefront

The data-informed leader needs to keep equity concerns at the forefront of data use efforts to ensure equitable learning opportunities for all students. Low-income students of color often lack access to high-quality, well-resourced schooling in the United States. The recent downturn in the economy led to a further decline in opportunities. School reform efforts have been halted in many places as time for teaching professional development was eliminated and teaching staff was reduced. At the same time that these school resources are being diminished, the number of youth who are struggling with homelessness, job losses among their parents, and difficulties meeting basic needs are growing. These conditions are compounded by a decrease in social welfare and health services provided by governmental and nongovernmental agencies.

The data-informed leader plays an important role in developing teachers' sense of ownership for improving the achievement of all of their students. Data can be used to address teachers' or leaders' low expectations of students from low-income or racially and ethnically diverse backgrounds in cases where this is an issue. Changing mind-sets takes considerable time, and thus the data-informed leader needs to stay the course in helping teachers confront assumptions about students that may pose barriers in improving achievement. Sharing data from schools or classrooms in the district where diverse students are achieving at high levels can help convince teachers that they can have similar success with their students.

Keeping equity concerns on the front burner requires careful attention to how data are used to plan instructional interventions for students. Thoughtful use of data could lead to flexible grouping and individualized learning plans that promote achievement for all students. However, with the documented rise in ability grouping over the past twenty years, it is possible that the use of accountability data to focus on students' varied proficiency rates has provided justification for grouping struggling students.[7] Misinformed or misguided use of data could also lead to increases in long-term ability grouping, which has been shown to widen the achievement gap between white students and students of color.[8] The data-informed leader must be ever attentive to these issues in order to ensure that all students are provided with opportunities to achieve at high levels in rigorous and engaging instruction.

Call #7: Center Data Use around Improving Instructional Practice

Centering data use around instructional practice is imperative for the data-informed leader who aims to improve education for all students. The real power in data-informed decision making is the ability to change classroom practice. In fact, this reform is premised on the idea that teachers who are guided by data are

The real power in data-informed decision making is the ability to change classroom practice.

better able to craft lessons to meet their students' needs. At the school level, leaders who draw on data will be able to make more informed decisions that ultimately improve classroom practice. As with a

focus on continuous improvement, the key to success here is thoughtful and systematic inquiry around multiple sources of data.

Many teachers work very hard to be thoughtful about the use of data to inform their instruction. They examine benchmark assessment data using their districts' data management systems and develop their own methods for monitoring student achievement using technology or simple pen and paper recording. They implement and draw on results from daily assessments that give them a barometer of student understanding. They look carefully at multiple sources of data on virtually everything students do in their classes: formal assessments, tests, quizzes, homework, essays, observations of student engagement during lessons, and so on. In many ways, this is just good teaching practice that is guided by formative assessment.[9] These teachers use varied types of data to create a complete picture of their students' achievement and creatively plan lessons to suit their students' diverse needs.

What is perhaps most important in this process of looking at data is the opportunity to pause, reflect, and sometimes gather more data before making decisions about instructional changes. This relates directly to call #1: building a culture of inquiry. This can be a challenge because research studies find that teachers' examination of data tends to be cursory rather than deep and focused on students' conceptual understanding. Teachers' data analysis tends to be simple and focused on gaining an understanding of students' strengths and weaknesses in order to reteach discrete skills.[10] Teachers must dig to find the underlying causes of achievement patterns, whether for an individual student, a group of students, or the whole class; they must not make hasty decisions that could potentially be harmful rather than helpful. Once teachers notice patterns in student achievement that require reteaching, they can brainstorm new methodologies and consult with colleagues for ideas. With experimentation, they can gather information on methods that might produce improved student engagement with the material or increased motivation.

When practice improves at the classroom level, there is a great likelihood that student learning will improve. As we have known for a long time but perhaps too easily forget, reforms must address the core processes of teaching and learning if they are to markedly change what happens in schools.[11] Some might argue that in the current policy moment, the decision-making powers of teachers have been diminished. That may be true at some level, but ultimately teachers' actions in the classroom are what matter most in educational reform. Teachers actively engage with reform agendas, passively accept them, or reject them, often in ways that are shaped by their work contexts and professional understandings.[12] The goal is for teachers to see such change in teaching and learning as a result of careful analysis of multiple forms of data on student achievement that they proudly proclaim, "I don't know what I ever did without these data!"

Facing the Future with Bold Leadership

The field of education in the United States is changing rapidly as we move toward more authentic assessments for student learning, an increased use of technology, and a greater focus on higher-order and critical thinking skills, among other twenty-first-century learning goals. Teachers and administrators are confronted by multiple new demands and pressures. These shifts bring new possibilities and challenges in the world of data use, especially as we broaden what constitutes data on student learning. Data-informed leadership will be ever more important in this new era.

This is our advice to data-informed leaders:

- Be bold and future oriented. Resist the temptation to adopt quick fixes or jump to conclusions when analyzing data.

- Avoid triage, and use data to work toward long-term continuous improvement.

- If data use is truly going to improve teaching and student learning, then engagement in reflective practice is imperative.

- Act when the evidence is clear and compelling rather than selectively choosing data points to make a case.

- When action is warranted, do not simply adopt wholesale what has worked well in another school. One-size-fits-all prescriptions for educational change have never been effective.

- Analyze why something has worked well and carefully identify what lessons can be drawn. Then replicate the principles rather than just the practices.

- Consider in advance how people will respond to new ways of working and anticipate potential problems.

- Continually gather data to examine whether data-informed leadership is leading to significant improvements.

Let's use data to ensure that all children truly have the learning opportunities to achieve their dreams.

Appendix:
Characteristics of Case Study
Schools and Districts

			Race/Ethnicity					Free Lunch Status	English Language Learner (ELL) Status
	Grades	Size	% African American	% Asian or Pacific Islander	% Latino	% White	% Native American	% Eligible	% ELL
District A	K–12	50,000	1	31	53	15	<1	60	47
School A	K–6	600	<1	72	11	17	<1	33	25
School B	K–6	1,200	1	25	67	8	<1	73	56
School C	9–12	1,600	<1	52	38	8	<1	67	42
District B	9–12	15,000	8	3	42	44	3	60	10
School A	9–12	1,600	11	4	47	34	4	55	11
District C	Pre-K–12	58,000	32	2	61	6	<1	78	27
School A	9	900	20	2	73	5	0	78	12
School B	K–4	600	15	2	81	4	0	86	66

Note: Figures have been rounded. They reflect demographics of sites during the study period (2006–2007 or 2007–2008).

Notes

Chapter 1: The Promise and Pitfalls of Data-Driven Decision Making

1. V. Mayer-Schonberger and K. Cukier, *Big Data: A Revolution That Will Transform How We Live, Work, and Think* (New York: Houghton Mifflin, 2003).

2. K. Schildkamp and M. K. Lai, "Introduction," in *Data-Based Decision Making in Education: Challenges and Opportunities*, ed. K. Schildkamp, M. K. Lai, and L. Earl (Dordrecht, Netherlands: Springer), 1–9.

3. N. R. Hoover and L. M. Abrams, "Teachers' Instructional Use of Summative Student Assessment Data," *Applied Measurement in Education* 26 (2013): 219–231; U.S. Department of Education, Office of Planning, Evaluation and Policy Development, *Teachers' Ability to Use Data to Inform Instruction: Challenges and Supports* (Washington, DC: Department of Education, 2010).

4. A. C. Dowd, *Data Don't Drive: Building a Practitioner-Driven Culture of Inquiry to Assess Community College Performance* (Boston: University of Massachusetts, Lumina Foundation for Education, 2005); Knapp et al. (2007).

5. We are indebted to Andy Hargreaves for this insight.

6. Mayer-Schonberger and Cukier (2013).

7. A. Hargreaves, "The Fourth Way of Change: Towards an Age of Inspiration and Sustainability" (unpublished manuscript, 2009), 9. See also A. Hargreaves and D. Shirley, *The Fourth Way: The Inspiring Future of Educational Change* (Thousand Oaks, CA: Corwin Press, 2009).

8. M. Rich, "Scandal in Atlanta Reignites Debate over Tests' Role," *New York Times*, April 2, 2013, A13.

9. G. Biesta, "Why 'What Works' Won't Work: Evidence Based Practice and the Democratic Deficit in Educational Research," *Educational Theory, 57*, no. 1 (2007): 1–23.

10. D. Shirley and A. Hargreaves, "Data-Driven to Distraction: Why American Educators Need a Reform Alternative—Where They Might Look to Find It," *Education Week*, October 4, 2006, 2–3, http://www.edweek.org/ew/articles/2006/10/04/06/hargreaves.h26.html.

11. D. Gillborn and D. Youdell, *Rationing Education: Policy, Practice, Reform and Equality* (Buckingham, England: Open University Press, 2000).

12. J. Booher-Jennings, "Below the Bubble: 'Educational Triage' and the Texas Accountability System," *American Educational Research Journal 42* (2005): 241.

13. Booher-Jennings (2005); A. Hargreaves and H. Braun, *Leading for All* (Ontario: Code Special Education Project, 2005).

14. J. Neumann, "Teaching to and beyond the Test: The Influence of Mandated Accountability Testing in One Social Studies Teacher's Classroom," *Teachers College Record, 115*, no. 6 (2013): 1–32.

15. R. Halverson, J. Grigg, R. Prichett, and C. Thomas, "The New Instructional Leadership: Creating Data-Driven Instructional Systems in Schools," working paper 2005–9 (Madison: Wisconsin Center for Education Research, 2005).

16. D. Light, M. Honey, J. Heinze, C. Brunner, D. Wexler, E. Mandinach, and C. Fasca, *Linking Data and Learning: The Grow Network Study* (New York: Educational Development Center, 2005).

17. J. B. Diamond and K. Cooper, "The Uses of Testing Data in Urban Elementary Schools: Some Lessons from Chicago," *Yearbook of the National Society for the Study of Education* 106 (2007): 241–263.

18. J. S. Wills and J. H. Sandholtz, "Constrained Professionalism: Dilemmas of Teaching in the Face of Test-Based Accountability," *Teachers College Record* 111 (2009): 1065–1114.

19. J. A. Marsh, J. A. Pane, and L. S. Hamilton, *Making Sense of Data-Driven Decision Making in Education: Evidence from Recent RAND Research* (Santa Monica, CA: RAND Education, 2006).

20. G. S. Ikemoto and J. A. Marsh, "Cutting through the 'Data Driven' Mantra: Different Conceptions of Data-Driven Decision Making," *Yearbook of the National Society for the Study of Education, 106* (2007): 105–131.

21. D. Ingram, K. S. Louis, and R. G. Schroeder, "Accountability Policies and Teacher Decision-Making: Barriers to the Use of Data to Improve Practice," *Teachers College Record* 106 (2004): 1258–1287; V. Park, "Beyond the Numbers Chase: How Urban High School Teachers Make Sense of Data Use" (PhD diss., University of Southern California, Rossier School of Education, 2008).

22. J. Feldman and R. Tung, "Whole School Reform: How Schools Use the Data-Based Inquiry and Decision Making Process" (paper presented at the annual meeting of the American Educational Research Association, Seattle, WA, 2001); Light et al. (2005).

23. J. Armstrong and K. Anthes, *Identifying the Factors, Conditions, and Policies That Support Schools' Use of Data for Decision Making and School Improvement: Summary of Findings* (Denver: Education Commission of the States, 2001); J. A. Supovitz and V. Klein, *Mapping a Course for Improved Student Learning: How Innovative Schools Systematically Use Student Performance Data to Guide Improvement* (Philadelphia: Consortium for Policy Research in Education, 2003); W. Togneri and S. Anderson, *Beyond Islands of Excellence: What Districts Can Do to Improve Instruction and Achievement in All Schools* (Washington, DC: Learning First Alliance, 2003).

24. J. W. Dembosky, J. F. Pane, H. Barney, and R. Christina, *Data Driven Decisionmaking in Southwestern Pennsylvania School Districts* (Santa Monica, CA: RAND, 2005), http://www.rand.org/pubs/working_papers/2006/RAND_WR326.pdf; J. A. Marsh, K. A. Kerr, G. S. Ikemoto, H. Darilek, M. Suttorp, R. W. Zimmer, and H. Barney, *The Role of Districts in Fostering Instructional Improvement: Lessons from Three Urban Districts Partnered with the Institute for Learning.* (Santa Monica, CA: RAND Corporation, 2005).

25. A. Datnow, V. Park, and P. Wohlstetter, *Achieving with Data: How High Performing School Systems Use Data to Improve Instruction for*

Elementary School Students (Los Angeles: Center on Educational Governance, 2007).

26. L. Earl and S. Katz, *Leading Schools in a Data-Rich World: Harnessing Data for School Improvement* (Thousand Oaks, CA: Corwin Press, 2006); Supovitz and Klein (2003).

27. E. Bensimon, "The Underestimated Significance of Practitioner Knowledge in the Scholarship of Student Success," *Review of Higher Education* 30 (2007): 441–469; V. Park, A. J. Daly, and A. W. Guerra, "Strategic Framing: How Leaders Craft the Meaning of Data Use for Equity and Learning," *Educational Policy* 27 (2013): 645–675; L. Skrla, J. J. Scheurich, and J. F. Johnson, *Equity-Driven Achievement-Focused School Districts* (Austin: Charles A. Dana Center, University of Texas at Austin, 2000), http://www.utdanacenter.org.

28. Armstrong and Anthes (2001).

29. Skrla et al. (2000).

30. M. A. Lachat and S. Smith, "Practices That Support Data Use in Urban High Schools," *Journal of Education for Students Placed at Risk* 10 (2005), 344–345.

31. V. L. Bernhardt, *Multiple Measures* (Oroville: California Association for Supervision and Curriculum Development, 1998).

32. Dowd (2005); J. Supovitz, "Can High Stakes Testing Leverage Educational Improvement? Prospects from the Last Decade of Testing and Accountability Reform," *Journal of Educational Change* 10 (2009): 211–227.

33. D. Rogosa, "Statistical Misunderstandings of the Properties of School Scores and School Accountability," in *Uses and Misuses of Data for Educational Accountability and Improvement*, ed. J. L. Herman and E. H. Haertel (Malden, MA: Blackwell, 2005), 147–174; Supovitz (2009).

34. B. L. Kennedy and A. Datnow, "Student Involvement and Data-Driven Decision Making: Developing a New Typology," *Youth and Society* 4 (2011): 1246–1271.

35. Feldman and Tung (2001); W. Togneri and S. Anderson, *Beyond Islands of Excellence: What Districts Can Do to Improve Instruction*

and Achievement in All Schools (Washington, DC: Learning First Alliance, 2003).

36. E. B. Mandinach and M. Honey, *Data-Driven School Improvement: Linking Data and Learning* (New York: Teachers College Press, 2008).

37. The Grow Network/McGraw-Hill Company online analytical tool provided teachers with an overview of student performance on New York state tests in math and English language arts and identified priority areas. The tool has been rebranded as the New York Statewide Testing and Accountability Reporting Tool. (See Mandanich & Honey, 2008, p. 155)

38. Ikemoto and Marsh (2007).

39. V. Park and A. Datnow, "Co-Constructing Distributed Leadership: District and School Connections in Data-Driven Decision Making," *School Leadership and Management* 29 (2009): 475–492.

40. M. S. Knapp, M. A. Copland, and J. A. Swinnerton, "Understanding the Promise and Dynamics of Data-Informed Leadership," *Yearbook of the National Society for the Study of Education* 106, no. 1 (2007): 74–104.

41. Mayer-Schonberger and Cukier (2013).

42. Park et al. (2013).

43. P. Gronn, "Distributed Properties: A New Architecture for Leadership," *Educational Management and Administration* 28 (2000): 317–338.

44. R. F. Elmore, "Hard Questions about Practice," *Educational Leadership* 59 (2002): 22–25; Gronn (2000); J. P. Spillane, R. Halverson, and J. Diamond, "Investigating School Leadership Practice: A Distributed Perspective," *Educational Researcher* 30, no. 23 (2001): 23–28.

45. K. A. Leithwood and C. Riehl, "What Do We Already Know about Educational Leadership?" in *A New Agenda for Research in Educational Leadership*, ed. W. A. Riehl and C. Riehl (New York: Teachers College Press, 2005), 12–27.

46. P. Gronn, "Leadership: Who Needs It?" *School Leadership and Management* 23 (2003): 267–290; J. P. Spillane, B. J. Reiser, and T. Reimer, "Policy Implementation and Cognition: Reframing and refocusing Implementation Research," *Review of Educational Research* 72 (2002): 387–431.

47. M. K. Stein and J. P. Spillane (2005), "What Can Researchers on Educational Leadership Learn from Research on Teaching? Building a Bridge," in W. A. Firestone and C. Riehl (eds.), *A New Agenda for Research in Educational Leadership* (New York: Teachers College Press), 28–45.

48. J. Spillane, R. Halverson, and J. B. Diamond (2004), "Towards a Theory of Leadership Practice: A Distributed Perspective," *Journal of Curriculum Studies* 36, no. 1 (2004): 3–34.

49. Gronn (2000).

50. R. F. Elmore, *Building a New Structure for School Leadership* (Washington, DC: Albert Shanker Institute, 2000); Spillane et al. (2004).

51. Spillane et al. (2004) focus on school-level practices. See also N. Bennett, C. Wise, P. A. Woods, and J. A. Harvey (2003), *Distributed Leadership: A Review of Literature* (Nottingham, England: National College of School Leadership), http://oro.open.ac.uk/8534/1/bennett-distributed-leadership-full.pdf.

52. Armstrong and Anthes (2001).

53. Armstrong and Anthes (2001).

54. M. Fullan, *Leading in a Culture of Change* (San Francisco: Jossey-Bass, 2001); P. Hallinger and R. H. Heck, "Reassessing the Principal's Role in School Effectiveness," *Educational Administration Quarterly* 32, no. 1 (1996): 5–44; K. Leithwood and D. Jantzi, "Transformational School Leadership for Large-Scale Reform: Effects on Students, Teachers, and Their Classroom Practices," *School Effectiveness and School Improvement* 17, no. 2 (2000): 201–227; J. Murphy and A. Datnow, *Leadership for School Reform: Lessons from Comprehensive School Reform Designs* (Thousand Oaks, CA: Corwin Press, 2003).

55. Armstrong and Anthes (2001); Datnow et al. (2007); Park and Datnow (2009); W. Togneri and S. E. Anderson, *Beyond Islands of Excellence: What Districts Can Do to Improve Instruction and Achievement in All Schools* (Washington, DC: Learning First Alliance, 2003).

Chapter 2: The Four Ps of Educational Reform

1. M. W. McLaughlin, "Learning from Experience: Lessons from Policy Implementation," *Educational Evaluation and Policy Analysis* 9 (1987): 171–178.

2. J. P. Spillane, "Data in Practice: Conceptualizing the Data-Based Decision-Making Phenomenon," *American Journal of Education* 118(2012): 114.

3. A. Datnow, L. Hubbard, and H. Mehan, *Extending Educational Reform: From One School to Many* (London and New York: Routledge/Farmer, 2002); A. Datnow and V. Park, "Conceptualizing Policy Implementation: Large-Scale Reform in an Era of Complexity," in *AERA Handbook on Education Policy Research*, ed. D. Plank, B. Schneider, and G. Sykes (New York: Routledge, 2009), 348–361.

4. J. P. Spillane, B. J. Reiser, and T. Reimer, "Policy Implementation and Cognition: Reframing and Refocusing Implementation Research," *Review of Educational Research* 72 (2002): 387–431.

5. C. E. Coburn, "Collective Sensemaking about Reading: How Teachers Mediate Reading Policy in Their Professional Communities," *Educational Evaluation and Policy Analysis* 23 (2001): 145–170.

6. Datnow and Park (2009).

7. W. A. Firestone, J. Fitz, and P. Broadfoot, "Power, Learning, and Legitimation: Assessment Implementation across Levels in the United States and the United Kingdom," *American Educational Research Journal* 36 (1999): 759–793; C. E. Coburn and J. E. Talbert, "Conceptions of Evidence Use in School Districts: Mapping the Terrain," *American Journal of Education* 112 (2006): 469–495.

8. A. Hargreaves and M. Fullan, *Professional Capital* (New York: Teachers College Press, 2012).

9. Hargreaves and Fullan (2012).

10. K. Leithwood, *Characteristics of High Performing School Districts: A Review of Empirical Evidence* (Calgary: College of Alberta School

Superintendents, 2008); G. Cawelti and G. Protheroe, "The School Board and Central Office in School Improvement," in *Handbook on Restructuring and Substantial School Improvement*, ed. H. Walberg (Lincoln, IL: Center on Innovation and Improvement, 2007), 37–52.

11. R. Yin, *Case Study Research*, 5th ed. (Beverly Hills, CA: Sage, 2013).

12. Yin (2013).

Chapter 3: Reculturing for Data Use

1. A. Hargreaves, *Changing Teachers, Changing Times* (New York: Teachers College Press, 1994).

2. M. I. Honig and M. A. Copland, *Reinventing District Central Offices to Expand Student Learning* (Washington, DC: Center for Comprehensive School Reform and Improvement, 2008).

3. A. Rorrer, L. Skrla, and J. A. Scheurich, "Districts as Institutional Actors in Educational Reform," *Educational Administration Quarterly* 44 (2008): 307–358.

4. B. Levin, A. Datnow, and N. Carrier, *Changing District Practices* (Boston: Jobs for the Future, 2012).

5. G. S. Ikemoto and J. A. Marsh, "Cutting through the 'Data Driven' Mantra: Different Conceptions of Data-Driven Decision Making," *Yearbook of the National Society for the Study of Education* 106 (2007): 105–131.

6. D. Ingram, K. S. Louis, and R. G. Schroeder, "Accountability Policies and Teacher Decision-Making: Barriers to the Use of Data to Improve Practice," *Teachers College Record* 106 (2004): 1258–1287.

7. L. Earl and M. Fullan, "Using Data in Leadership for Learning," *Cambridge Journal of Education* 33 (2003): 383–394.

8. L. Skrla and J. Scheurich, "Displacing Deficit Thinking," *Education and Urban Society* 33 (2001): 235–259.

9. J. Murphy, S. N. Elliot, E. Goldring, and A. C. Porter, *Learning-Centered Leadership: A Conceptual Foundation* (Nashville, TN: Vanderbilt Learning Sciences Institute, 2006).

10. V. Park and A. Datnow, "Co-Constructing Distributed Leadership: District and School Connections in Data-Driven Decision Making," *School Leadership and Management* 29 (2009): 475–492.

11. Honig and Copland (2008), 3.

12. S. Sarason, *The Predictable Failure of Educational Reform* (San Francisco: Jossey-Bass, 1990); M. Fullan, *The New Meaning of Educational Change* (New York: Teachers College Press, 1991).

13. E. Foley and D. Sigler, "Getting Smarter: A Framework for Districts," *Voices in Urban Education* 22 (2009): 5–12.

14. N. Protheroe, "District Support for School Improvement," *Principal* 87 (2008): 36–39.

Chapter 4: Goals, Routines, and Tools for Data Use

1. J. P. Spillane, "Data in Practice: Conceptualizing the Data-Based Decision-Making Phenomenon," *American Journal of Education* 118 (2012): 114.

2. I. S. Horn and J. W. Little, "Attending to Problems of Practice: Routines and Resources for Professional Learning in Teachers' Workplace Interactions," *American Educational Research Journal*, 47, no. 1 (2010): 181–217.

3. L. Hamilton, R. Halverson, S. S. Jackson, E. Mandinach, J. Supovitz, and J. Wayman, *Using Student Achievement Data to Support Instructional Decision Making*, IES practice guide, NCEE 2009–4067 (Washington, DC: National Center for Education Evaluation and Regional Assistance, 2009).

4. M. I. Honig and N. Venkateswaran, "School-Central Office Relationships in Evidence Use: Understanding Evidence Use as a Systems Problem," *American Journal of Education* 118 (2012): 199–222; E. B. Mandinach and M. Honey (eds.), *Data Driven*

School Improvement: Linking Data and Learning (New York: Teachers College Press, 2008); B. Means, C. Padilla, and L. Gallagher, *Use of Education Data at the Local Level: From Accountability to Instructional Improvement* (Washington, DC: US Department of Education, Office of Planning, Evaluation, and Policy Development, 2010).

5. Horn and Little (2010); V. M. Young, "Teachers' Use of Data: Loose Coupling, Agenda Setting, and Team Norms," *American Journal of Education* 112 (2006): 521–548.

6. A. Hargreaves, *Changing Teachers, Changing Times* (New York: Teachers College Press, 1994); G. Kelchtermans, "Teacher Collaboration and Collegiality as Workplace Conditions: A Review," *Zeitschrift fur Padagogik* 2 (2006): 220–237.

7. See A. J. Daly, "Data, Dyads, and Dynamics: Exploring Data Use and Social Networks in Educational Improvement," *Teachers College Record 114* (2012): 1–38.

8. Horn and Little (2010).

9. J. B. Christman, R. C. Neild, K. Bulkley, S. Blanc, R. Liu, C. Mitchell, and E. Travers. "Making the Most of Interim Assessment Data. Lessons from Philadelphia." Research for action (2009).

10. Hargreaves (1994).

11. Hargreaves (1994), 248.

12. L. Anderson and D. A. Krathwohl, *Taxonomy for Learning, Teaching and Assessing: A Revision of Bloom's Taxonomy of Educational Objectives* (New York: Longman, 2001).

13. L. Lezotte and K. M. McKee, *Assembly Required: A Continuous School Improvement System* (Okemus, MI: Effective Schools Products, 2002).

14. A. Lieberman and L. Miller, *Teachers in Professional Communities: Improving Teaching and Learning* (New York: Teachers College Press, 2008).

15. C. E. Coburn and M. K. Stein (eds.), *Research and Practice in Education: Building Alliances, Bridging the Divide* (Lanham, MD: Rowman and Littlefield, 2010).

16. G. S. Ikemoto and M. Honig, "Tools to Deepen Practitioners' Engagement with Research: The Case of the Institute for Learning," in *Research and Practice in Education: Building Alliances, Bridging the Divide*, ed. C. E. Coburn and M. K. Stein (Lanham, MD: Rowman and Littlefield, 2010), 95.

Chapter 5: Using Data for Instructional Improvement

1. K. A. Samaniego, "Case Studies of Teacher Perceptions and Their Enactment Processes When Implementing Multiple Reforms in Urban High School Mathematics" (PhD diss., University of California, San Diego, 2013).

2. J. A. Supovitz and V. Klein, *Mapping a Course for Improved Student Learning: How Innovative Schools Systematically Use Student Performance Data to Guide Improvement* (Philadelphia: Consortium for Policy Research in Education, 2003).

3. M. Heritage, "Formative Assessment: What Do Teachers Need to Know and Do?" *Phi Delta Kappan* 89 (2007): 141–142.

4. P. Black, C. Harrison, C. Lee, B. Marshall, and D. Wiliam, *Assessment for Learning* (Berkshire, England: Open University Press, 2003); P. Black and D. Wiliam, "Developing a Theory of Formative Assessment," in *Assessment and Learning*, ed. J. R. Gardner (London: Sage, 2006), 81–100; Heritage (2007); J. L. Herman, E. Osmundson, C. Ayala, S. Schneider, and M. Timms, "The Nature and Impact of Teachers' Formative Assessment Practices," technical report 703 (Los Angeles: Center for the Study of Evaluation, 2006); S. Leahy, C. Lyon, M. Thompson, and D. Wiliam, "Classroom Assessment: Minute by Minute, Day by Day," *Educational Leadership* 63 (2005): 18–24, http://www2.esu3.org/esu3/workshopDocs/Article.pdf; M. A. Ruiz-Primo and E. M. Furtak, "Exploring Teachers' Informal Formative Assessment Practices and Students' Understanding of the Context of Scientific Inquiry," *Journal of Research in Science Teaching* 44, no. 1 (2007): 57–84, http://www3.interscience.wiley.com/cgi-bin/fulltext/113510306/PDFSTART.

5. L. Earl and S. Katz, *Leading Schools in a Data-Rich World: Harnessing Data for School Improvement* (Thousand Oaks, CA: Corwin Press, 2006).

6. J. A. Marsh, K. A. Kerr, G. S. Ikemoto, H. Darilek, M. Suttorp, R. W. Zimmer, and H. Barney, *The Role of Districts in Fostering Instructional Improvement: Lessons from Three Urban Districts Partnered with the Institute for Learning.* (Santa Monica, CA: RAND, 2005); S. Mason, "Turning Data into Knowledge: Lessons from Six Milwaukee Public Schools" (paper presented at the annual meeting of the American Educational Research Association, New Orleans, LA, 2002); L. Petrides and T. Nodine, *Anatomy of School System Improvement: Performance-Driven Practices in Urban School Districts* (San Francisco: NewSchools Venture Fund, 2005).

7. J. Feldman and R. Tung, "Whole School Reform: How Schools Use The Data-Based Inquiry and Decision Making Process" (paper presented at the annual meeting of the American Educational Research Association, Seattle, WA, 2001); Mason (2002); Supovitz and Klein (2003).

8. Heritage (2007).

9. See www.avid.org for more information on the program.

Chapter 6: Facing the Future with Data-Informed Leadership

1. G. S. Ikemoto and J. A. Marsh, "Cutting through the 'Data Driven' Mantra: Different Conceptions of Data-Driven Decision Making," *Yearbook of the National Society for the Study of Education*, 106 (2007): 105–131.

2. J. P. Spillane, "Data in Practice: Conceptualizing the Data-Based Decision-Making Phenomenon," *American Journal of Education* 118 (2012): 114.

3. M. S. Knapp, M. A. Copland, and J. A. Swinnerton, "Understanding the Promise and Dynamics of Data-Informed Leadership," *Yearbook for the National Society for the Study of Education* 106, no. 1 (2007): 74–104, doi:10.1111/j.1744–7984.2007.00098.x.

4. A. Hargreaves and M. Fullan, *Professional Capital* (New York: Teachers College Press, 2012).

5. C. E. Coburn, "Collective Sensemaking about Reading: How Teachers Mediate Reading Policy in Their Professional Communities," *Educational Evaluation and Policy Analysis* 23 (2001): 145–170.

6. Hargreaves and Fullan (2012), 93–94.

7. Loveless, *The 2013 Brown Center Report on American Education: How Well Are American Students Learning?* Vol. 3, no. 2 (Washington, DC: Brookings, 2013), http://www.brookings.edu/2013-brown-center-report.

8. J. Oakes, *Keeping Track: How Schools Structure Inequality* (New Haven, CT: Yale University Press, 1985); J. Schofield, "International Evidence on Ability Grouping with Curriculum Differentiation and the Achievement Gap in Secondary Schools," *Teachers College Record* 112 (2010): 8–9.

9. R. J. Stiggins and J. Chappuis, "What a Difference a Word Makes: Assessment for Learning Rather Than Assessment of Learning Helps Students Succeed," *Journal of Staff Development* 27 (2006): 10–14.

10. N. R. Hoover and L. M. Abrams, "Teachers' Instructional Use of Summative Student Assessment Data," *Applied Measurement in Education* 26 (2013): 219–231 L. N. Oláh, N. R. Lawrence, and M. Riggan, "Learning to Learn from Benchmark Assessment Data: How Teachers Analyze Results," *Peabody Journal of Education* 85 (2010): 226–245; V. Park, "Beyond the Numbers Chase: How Urban High School Teachers Make Sense of Data Use" (PhD diss., University of Southern California, Rossier School of Education, 2008).

11. R. Elmore, "Getting to Scale with Good Educational Practice," *Harvard Educational Review* 66, no. 1 (1996): 1–26.

12. Coburn (2001); B. Olsen and D. Sexton, "Threat Rigidity, School Reform, and How Teachers View Their Work inside Current Education Policy Contexts," *American Educational Research Journal* 46, no. 1 (2009): 9–44.

Index

Ability grouping, 125

Accountability policies: of case study sites, 39–41; data use and, 3–7; data-informed decision making and, 12; goal setting related to, 71–75; perverse incentives of, 3–7, 117–118; as political leverage, 33, 40, 41, 117–118; for reducing achievement gaps, 3–4, 5–6

Accountability pressures: adverse effects of, 122; for case study sites, 39–41; framing data use with trust *versus*, 47, 48–49, 56, 57–59, 120–121; of No Child Left Behind, 39, 40; state tests and, 39–43

Achievement gaps: accountability policies for reducing, 3–4, 5–6; creating high expectations to overcome, 60–62, 64–65; data use for understanding and remedying, 95–99, 124–125

Achievement Via Individual Determination (AVID) strategies, 113

Action plans: advice for, 128; data use for, 96–97; student-written, 107; writing and revising, 72–73, 74, 123

Adequate Yearly Progress (AYP) deadlines, 5

Administrators: case study interviews with, 35, 36; data use role of, 20, 21; linkages between district and school, 47, 121; professional development role of, 113–114; student engagement improvement role of, 106. *See also* Superintendents

Affective elements, 108, 109

Analysis-focused schools, 15

Assessments: classroom-level, 98, 99–101, 114–115; formative, 84, 98, 99–101, 112; limited relevance of, 57, 63–64, 108–110; measuring goals with, 99–101; multiple forms of, 84, 98, 99–101, 123, 126; range of, in case study sites, 42. *See also* Benchmark assessments; State tests

Attendance records, 10

Australia, 2

Belgium, 2

Beliefs, changing culture and, 46–47, 62–65. *See also* Reculturing

Benchmark assessments: alignment of, to Common Core State Standards, 69; alignment of, to state tests, 69, 74–76, 82–83; in case study sites, 41; combining other assessments with, 98, 99–101, 126; data management system access to, 69, 81, 85–86; development of, 80–82; to identify students with needs, 65, 82–83, 84; involvement in, 80–81, 84; lessons about, 84; overview of, 69; pacing and, 67–68; questions about, 94; teacher perceptions of, 80–84; timing of, 82; use of, 10, 80–84, 123–124; usefulness of, 82–84

Boldness, 128

Boston's New England Aquarium, 119

"Bubble kids," 5–6, 118

Canada, 2

Capacity, for data use: building, 110–114, 121–122; complexity levels and, 15–17; learning framework for, 12, 14. *See also* Professional development; Skill building

Case study, 31–43; accountability policies in sites of, 39–41; data collection for, 35–37; first phase of (school districts), 34; four Ps framework in, 37–43; framework for data-informed decision making used in, 31–33; instructional improvement in, 97–115; leaders in sites of, 37–39; overview of, 22, 31–33; patterns in sites of, 41–43; policy context of sites in, 39–41; practices in sites of, 41–43; reculturing in, 49–65; second phase of (schools), 34–35; site demographics in, 35, 130; site features in, 37–43; site selection for, 33–35; tools and routines in, 69–94

Change: incremental approach to, 38, 50, 113; leading the process of, 49–52, 121, 128

Cheating, on state tests, 3–4, 118

Check-ins, 100–101, 115

Classroom: assessments, 98, 99–101, 114–115, 126; management, 102–103; practices, 101–104, 114

Coaches, 113